# I Remember My Teacher

# I Remember My Teacher

## 365 Reminiscences of the Teachers Who Changed Our Lives

DAVID M. SHRIBMAN

**Andrews McMeel
Publishing**

Kansas City

# I Remember My Teacher

02 03 04 05 QUF 10 9 8 7 6 5 4

Library of Congress Cataloging-in-Publication Data
I remember my teacher : 365 reminiscences of the teachers who changed our lives / [compiled by] David M. Shribman.
    p. cm.
  ISBN 0-7407-2203-4
    1. Teachers—Biography. 2. Coaches (Athletics)—Biography. I. Shribman, David M.

LA2301 .I22 2001
371.1'0092'2—dc21

               2001045776

Book design and composition by Holly Camerlinck

To teachers, unforgettable and unappreciated alike, the men and women who taught us how to think, to create, to dream—and, as this book shows, to remember.

# Preface

*I* remember Mr. DiMento, who made me memorize all fifteen of the Soviet Socialist Republics, and I remember his brother, who made me memorize the quadratic formula. I don't remember a thing about the Kazakh Soviet Socialist Republic or the quadratic equation, but I remember a lot about the discipline of learning, which I now know was their real lesson.

I remember Miss Waterman, who taught about the life cycle of the butterfly, which I still remember, and about life itself, which I still haven't mastered. I remember Professor Gelfant, who taught college students how to read for the first time.

I remember Mrs. Rich, who in a terrible November in 1963 tried to explain the inexplicable to unbelieving fourth-graders. I remember Miss Koury, who introduced me to Aaron Copland and who taught an enduring lesson to the tune of "Simple Gifts."

I remember the Miss White who taught Dickens and the Miss White who taught trigonometry. I remember Mr. Michaels, who taught world history, and Mrs. Michaels, who taught French.

I remember Mr. Kimball, who had the audacity to think that the Missouri Compromise and the Spanish-American War were important, and Professor Wright, who lectured about Andrew Johnson and argued that knowing how a president was impeached might come in handy someday. I've never forgotten a thing either man ever said.

I remember Professor Slesnick. I never took one of his math classes. No one ever loved me more. I remember Coach Lupien. I never played an inning for him. No one ever taught me more.

I have watched (and worshiped) teachers for years. I have two sisters-in-law who are teachers (one math, one physics). I have two daughters who adore their teachers. I have learned very little in life, but I've learned enough to appreciate teachers.

So, apparently, have you. For a year I stopped everyone I encountered—insurance agents and airline ticket agents, diamond miners and coal miners, governors and senators, bakers and business executives, actors and accountants, engineers, lifeguards, anesthesiologists, judges, and pharmacists—and asked them to tell me about the teachers and coaches who changed their minds, changed their perspectives, and changed their lives.

Everyone had a story. Everyone had a teacher who made an impression—and who made a difference. Everyone remembered at least one person who proved that Henry Adams was right when he said that "a teacher affects eternity."

This book is a collection of stories and tributes, one for each day of the year. It is my way, and your way, of saying thank you. And of revising an old refrain. Let's agree: Those who can, do. Those who teach, do more.

—*David M. Shribman*

# *I Remember* . . .

*L*ennis Tedford. She was my piano teacher. She taught me Mozart to have fun, Czerny for discipline, Rachmaninoff to show off. She made me use the metronome so I could do things in an orderly way. She had gnarled, arthritic fingers and she couldn't play a note. But she brought the music out of me and lots of other kids in Maryville, Tennessee.

*—Lamar Alexander, former governor of Tennessee*

*W*hen I was six years old, my family had just emigrated here from Korea. I didn't speak any English. I had a Korean name that none of the other kids could pronounce. But there was one teacher who made sure she pronounced it right. Finally my parents recognized this problem. They got me to choose a nickname that all the other kids could pronounce. So I chose "Kathy." That was the teacher's name, and it is my legal name now.

*—Kathy Chung, communications department,*
*Democratic National Committee, Washington, D.C.*

# I Remember . . .

$\mathcal{M}$y math teacher at Cejep de Maisonneuve in Montreal. He taught us statistics with cards and dice. I even remember some of it.

*—Isobelle Lemelien, bookseller, Montreal, Quebec*

$\mathcal{T}$om Finch, who taught mining courses at Montana Tech. He was brash. He was a character. I didn't grow up in a mining town, but he was an old-time miner and he helped me understand what actually works in the real world and in the real mines in the Arctic, where I now work.

*—Adam Gould, field engineer, Diavik diamond mine,*
*Northwest Territories*

$\mathcal{M}$r. Edgel Sereno, my algebra teacher at Southern High School in Oakland, Maryland. He would put paper over the windows of the door and let us play poker.

*—Linda Freyman, physical education teacher, Accident, Maryland*

$\mathcal{B}$ob McCloskey, who taught constitutional law at Harvard. He told me it was not necessary to remember all of the facts about any subject—and that the thing I really needed to know was someone I could call who did know all the facts.

—*Sandy Maisel, political scientist, Waterville, Maine*

$\mathcal{J}$ohn Thomas Walker, who later became an Episcopal bishop. He was the first African-American teacher at St. Paul's School and he was concerned about politics and humanity. He taught me that a gentle person could be a strong person.

—*John F. Kerry, senator from Massachusetts*

$\mathcal{A}$ professor I had in a counseling education course during my Ph.D. program. He told me in no uncertain terms: I didn't have what it takes to be a psychologist.

—*Malcolm Rubinstein, psychologist, Winston-Salem, North Carolina*

# *I Remember . . .*

*A*lexander Lipsky. He was my piano teacher, and I will never forget when he got angry at me. I wasn't practicing enough and he gave me grief. He told me I was slacking off. He raised his voice. But—and this is the important thing—he made sure we were on good terms when the lesson ended. He showed me the difference between what I did, which wasn't much, and who I was, which was still something good.

—*Matthew Harre, piano teacher, Washington, D.C.*

*M*y professor John Bremner, a former Jesuit priest. He was the smartest man I've ever known. Once he assigned me a paper for a seminar. I knew when I turned it in that it wasn't very good, or good enough. He shamed me in front of the whole class. He looked directly at me and said: "Miss Walsh, this is a mediocre paper and you are not a mediocre person." I think of that all the time. He taught me that I was not a mediocre person.

—*Sharon Walsh, writer, New York, New York*

4

# *I Remember . . .*

*S*ister Mary Virgilius, my eighth-grade teacher at St. Benedict School in Savannah. She didn't coddle us. She wouldn't take no for an answer. She demanded the best and she got it.

—*Clarence Thomas, Supreme Court justice, Washington, D.C.*

*M*r. Ludtke. He was a history teacher at Massapequa High School on Long Island. He was young and fun. He taught me an important lesson: not to be afraid to learn.

—*Sue Hayes, administrative assistant, Salem, Massachusetts*

*M*rs. Nachman in second grade. One day I just wasn't paying attention. I must have been a little bored in class. She told me that whenever I wanted to go to the library I could go. I went a lot. I was never bored again.

—*George Stephanopoulos, former White House aide and television news personality, New York, New York*

# $\mathcal{I}$ $\mathcal{R}$emember . . .

$\mathcal{M}$iss Staples, my high school teacher in Winnipeg. It was years ago but I still remember how calm she was and how gently she talked to us.

—*Helen Otto, museum guide, Drumheller, Alberta*

$\mathcal{M}$y math teacher at Cohoes High School in upstate New York. He made algebra digestible. He kept everybody's attention. That's not easy with kids of algebra age.

—*Raymond LaMora, insurance agent, Elkins, West Virginia*

$\mathcal{T}$aking accelerated English in a Chicago public high school in 1957. We thought we were the smartest kids around and then we confronted Agnes Swindberg, a little lady with her hair in a bun. She looked like she was a hundred years old. And the first term she handed out the grades: No one got higher than a C. She taught us that we weren't as smart as we thought we were. I've tried to remember that since.

—*Lynn Martin, former secretary of labor, Chicago, Illinois*

# I Remember...

$\mathcal{B}$rooks Blossom, my Latin teacher in high school. This was supposed to be a dead language, but to Brooks Blossom, Latin was a language that was fully alive.

—*Michael Harris, stockbroker, Ogunquit, Maine*

$\mathcal{N}$ed Wulk, who was my teacher and coach in college. I consulted with him before I signed my baseball contract. He molded all the important decisions I made when I was young. He taught me an important lesson—that I had to control myself before I could control anything.

—*Jim Bunning, Kentucky senator and former major-league pitcher*

$\mathcal{S}$am Feller, the track coach at Woodrow Wilson High School. I had never run track before, but he talked me into doing it. A lot of coaches put themselves above us. He didn't. He came down to our level.

—*Jim Freedman, art framer, Washington, D.C.*

$\mathcal{H}$ilda MacGowan, my grade four teacher at the Liverpool Academy. She was just sweet and interesting. She was, to everyone, the same.

—*Lou Louthise, retired bookkeeper, Liverpool, Nova Scotia*

$\mathcal{M}$ary Kay Banner. She taught at Thaddeus Stevens Elementary School in Clarion, Pennsylvania. I thought she was really old at the time, but of course she wasn't. She played piano, and so we sang between classes. She was the best teacher I ever had because she was the happiest teacher I ever had.

—*Deborah Hamilton-Lynne, playwright, Austin, Texas*

$\mathcal{M}$r. Gutermuth, my sixth-grade teacher at Lincoln Elementary School in Ohio. He wasn't my favorite at the time. In fact, I hated him. He made our work really hard. He made us learn really hard stuff. Now I meet a lot of people who have never had a lot of rigor. I was lucky to have Mr. Gutermuth.

—*Janice Shields, writer, Washington, D.C.*

# $\mathscr{I}$ $\mathscr{R}$emember . . .

$\mathscr{M}$rs. Hodgkins. She was my English teacher in a rural school in Michigan. She taught me something I've never forgotten: that what I read and how I wrote would make a difference in how I lived my life.

*—John Engler, governor of Michigan*

$\mathscr{P}$rofessor Oliver Schroeder, who taught me in a constitutional-law class during summer school. It was a 7:40 class in the morning three days a week, and one of them was Saturday. And this guy came in with such energy, such excitement, such enthusiasm that I couldn't help but pay attention. I learned some constitutional law that summer, but I also learned that people respond in direct proportion to how much you reach out to them.

*—Donald Rumsfeld, secretary of defense, Washington, D.C.*

$\mathscr{G}$erald M. Kramer. I was a graduate student in periodontics at Boston University. He took a pretty insecure kid from humble beginnings and made me very secure with what I do every day.

*—Michael P. Stiglitz, periodontist, Washington, D.C.*

# *I Remember . . .*

*M*rs. Remmer. She was my English teacher at Brockville Collegiate Institute in Ontario. I think she had read everything, and she got us to read loads. I'm glad because she taught mostly Canadian novels, and no other teacher emphasized Canadian writers like she did.

—*Shannon Tayles, assistant dining-room manager, Jasper, Alberta*

*S*ister Patricia. She taught me in sophomore, junior, and senior years of high school in Mobile, Alabama. She told me something that I didn't understand until later, and it was advice that I didn't follow until later. She told me: "You can fly, but that cocoon has to go." I could, and it did.

—*Alexis Herman, former secretary of labor, Washington, D.C.*

*B*ogdan Tosic. When I was in grades four through eight he was my best teacher in Belgrade. He was strict and honest. I realized many years later that that was a good combination.

—*Hristo Cicanovski, pilot, Toronto, Ontario*

*I* grew up in the White House, but I also grew up in a deep search for the white picket fence, a bunch of kids, and a couple of dogs. I wanted them so badly that I never got my college degree. And later in life I encountered a woman named Pat Hayes, the president of St. Edward's University. She asked me a question: "Are you ever going to make room for Someday, are you ever going to make Someday work for you?" I decided Someday had arrived for me.

—*Luci Baines Johnson, college graduate at age fifty, Austin, Texas*

*Mr.* Cooper, who was my twelfth-grade English teacher at Melrose High School in Massachusetts. He had a no-nonsense approach to life. Before spring break in my senior year I started to grow a beard, mostly so I would look old enough to buy beer in Florida. He stopped mid-sentence one day and said, "You— shave that beard." I did.

—*Jim Puzzanghera, writer, Washington, D.C.*

# I Remember . . .

*B*ennett Meyers. He was the program director at Camp Winnebago in Maine, and when I was an older camper there I was involved in a ruse in a capture-the-flag game. Bennett was a pillar of integrity, unwavering in his morality. What had been my winning formula until then was to disarm critics with humor, humility, remorse, or manners—and to walk away scot-free. He would have none of that. He didn't shout. I wasn't punished. Worse than either, he expressed his disappointment in me as a leader and a captain. We became close friends and colleagues over the years. He attended my graduation from college. But the wound in my heart never completely healed. I had let Bennett Meyers down.

—*Phil Lilienthal, director, Camp Winnebago, Fayette, Maine*

*H*usham Sharabi, who taught nineteenth-century European intellectual history at Georgetown University. I had had fifteen years of Catholic education. He was a Palestinian Marxist. We had nothing in common. He made me question everything I thought, and he made me question every word I said and every word I wrote.

—*Timothy Aluise, lawyer, Washington, D.C.*

# $\mathscr{I}\ \mathscr{Remember}\dots$

$\mathscr{M}$r. Kaufman, my history teacher at Woburn High. He had a good time with us. He taught us not to take life too seriously.

—*Lisa Lee, American Airlines ticket agent, Boston, Massachusetts*

$\mathscr{A}$lden Poole, who taught freshman journalism at Simmons College. He was a crusty old newspaperman but he managed to make everything seem brand-new and fresh to us. He took a bunch of kids who had no idea what they wanted to do with their lives and made them believe they wanted to be newspaper reporters. It's not clear that he taught us a thing about journalism, but he taught me to love journalism.

—*Gwen Ifill, anchor of* Washington Week in Review,
*Shirlington, Virginia*

$\mathscr{M}$rs. Reid. She taught second grade in Hull, Quebec. She was a very special teacher. She said one thing I've never forgotten. She told us that a rainbow was God's ring.

—*Henrietta Forbes, child-care provider, Edmonton, Alberta*

# *I Remember . . .*

*A*rthur Funston, who taught me in my sophomore year at Earlham College in Richmond, Indiana. We were reading Plato and Machiavelli in class, and I was involved in the college news-paper, staying up all night and not reading political philosophy. One day he singled me out and said, "Don, could you see me after class?" I thought I was cooked, and I was ready to get reamed out. I sat in his office and he asked me whether I wanted to be a college professor—he said it was a profession where you could study what you wanted and have the pleasure of sharing it with others—and when I kind of muttered that that might be pretty good he gave me some advice: "If you want to teach, you have to do the reading."

—*Donald McNemar, president, Guilford College,
Greensboro, North Carolina*

*J*ames W. Carey, a professor I had in journalism school at Illinois. He was a very committed intellectual and a lively personality. I wasn't particularly bookish. But he had an ability to encourage me to see the world in a much larger way. He taught me not how to write a coherent lead but how to live a coherent life.

—*Dan Balz, chief political writer,* The Washington Post

# *I Remember . . .*

*My* third-grade teacher. Her name was Jean Duren. She was unfailingly positive, and she told us always to look for the positive. You know, I still do.

—*Ron Colvin, former teacher, Washington, D.C.*

*Mr.* Murdock. He taught math at Cameron Heights Collegiate in Kitchener, Ontario. To him, teaching was not a job.

—*Ross Hagen, conservation officer, Fort Laird, Northwest Territories*

*Mrs.* Stone, my art teacher at Abington Friends School. I thought of her as an "older person," but then again, I was in the second grade. She let me believe I had artistic talent—and that it was okay to color outside the lines. I remember printmaking with potatoes, making Easter eggs from sugar and L'eggs pantyhose shells and making those doll heads from apples that shrink up to look like very old people. And now that I have a son, I look forward to doing some of Mrs. Stone's old projects with him—and to teaching him it's okay to color outside the lines.

—*Caren Orlick Korin, account consultant, DaVor Photography,*
*Boston, Massachusetts*

# $\mathcal{I}$ $\mathcal{R}$*emember* . . .

$\mathcal{M}$iss Newburry, my English teacher at York Mills Collegiate. She liked her subject. I'm not a big fan of American literature, but I still remember the American literature she taught. She made it unforgettable. I still don't know how she made Faulkner interesting.

—*Jim Clarke, passenger agent, Toronto, Ontario*

$\mathcal{D}$ouglas Perkins. He was the journalism teacher at Northside Rural High, north of San Antonio. My father was a journalist, but I had never given any thought to being a reporter. Mr. Perkins taught me about reporting, and every night I would come home and tell my father how to be a reporter. Mr. Perkins made me interested in journalism. But he also made me interested in my father.

—*Deborah Howell, Washington, D.C., bureau chief,*
*Newhouse News Service*

$\mathcal{W}$ally Mlyniec, my law school prof at Georgetown. He was intense beyond belief. He made us do moot court. He made us dress right. He made us look through police reports. There was one case in moot court I simply did not want to do. I would have done anything to avoid it. And he made sure—he went out of his way—to make sure I got that case. He did it because he knew it would teach me something, and it did.

—*Amy Friend, lawyer, Washington, D.C.*

$\mathcal{M}$iss Heldegarde Biskey. She opened each day of third grade with a book, an anthology of poetry. She told us to close our eyes as we listened to the poem of the day. At first the poems were short, but as the year progressed they grew longer. In high school I learned the finer points of poetry mechanics: the difference between a sonnet and a ballade, the humor of alliteration, the rhythms of iambic pentameter. But it was never as fun, or as free, as it was with Miss Biskey. She introduced us to the beauty of words and taught us that life is poetry.

—*Nancy Kepes Jeton, urban planner, Andover, Massachusetts*

# *I Remember . . .*

*M*y high school biology teacher, Mr. Lipsig. He was a young guy with a loosened tie, a lay teacher in a Catholic school. He used to tell us that sex was re-creation, not recreation. Coming from a cool guy, that meant something.

—*Andrew Cuomo, former secretary of housing and urban development, New York, New York*

*M*y ninth-grade English teacher. She challenged us like crazy. To this day I still have the vocabulary book she made us study. Because of her, I learned words like *intrepid* and *arduous* before I had to.

—*Don Siegelman, governor of Alabama*

*M*ary Powers. I grew up in Cumming, Iowa, and I came from a family where my father had an eighth-grade education and my mother was an immigrant who could barely read English. I remember that when I went to school Mrs. Powers opened a book and read a story to me. No one had ever done that for me before.

—*Tom Harkin, U.S. senator, Cumming, Iowa*

*G*il Henry. He taught auto-body repair at the College of Trades and Technology in St. John's, Newfoundland. He knew the insides of an automobile and a little bit more.

—*Fred Chafe, heavy-equipment mechanic, Lumsden, Newfoundland*

*M*other Mouton. She was the headmistress of the Convent of the Sacred Heart, where I went to school. It was a place where it was very important to be quiet all the time. You had to be quiet in the halls, quiet in class. But even so, Mother Mouton used to say: Silence is golden—but sometimes it is just plain yellow.

—*Kathleen Kennedy Townsend, lieutenant governor of Maryland*

*M*y tenth-grade English teacher. He used to give us compositions to write, but he would give us specific subjects. I didn't write on the subjects he gave us. Rather than give me an F he said he appreciated my creativity. I remember him because he didn't squelch me.

—*Rob Reiner, film director*

# I Remember . . .

Robert Dozier, who taught math at West Virginia University. He told me that history, English, and political science were whatever the teacher wanted to make them but that mathematics was one and one is two. He helped me see the simplicity in complexity.

*—Jim Shimbo, ski instructor, Elkins, West Virginia*

Mr. Shaughnessy, my freshman English teacher at North Catholic High School in Troy Hill in Pittsburgh. He was a bachelor, he wore the same suit every day, and he smelled terrible. He made us diagram sentences. He taught a class full of boys the basics.

*—Tom Devlin, consultant, McLean, Virginia*

Mrs. Price, my first-grade teacher. She encouraged me to really get into reading. And she used to take me around the classroom to help other kids to read. She pushed me to do two things: to read and to help others. I've tried to do a lot of both.

*—Rodney Slater, former secretary of transportation, Washington, D.C.*

# $\mathcal{I}$ $\mathcal{R}$emember . . .

$\mathcal{T}$eresa Tigani, my grade six teacher at Brebuf Junior High School in Calgary. She was so good. You could joke around with her. You could play any prank on her and not get in trouble.

—*Sylvana Lau, flight attendant, Calgary, Alberta*

$\mathcal{J}$ohn Tobias Conway. He was like a second father to me. He was a history teacher, but he was also the baseball coach at New London High School. I was his baseball manager for three years. One day I used the phrase "my old lady" in reference to my mother. He said: "Johnny, she is your mother. Never, ever refer to her as an old lady." I never did that again.

—*John J. DeGange, consultant, Lebanon, New Hampshire*

$\mathcal{C}$oach Barton. He was a baseball coach and a government teacher. He was a thoroughly '60s guy, and I was living in rural Virginia at the time. He made me interested in government at a time in my life when I wasn't interested in anything.

—*Bill Brough, political activist, Alexandria, Virginia*

*S*arah Shaffer, my fifth-grade teacher at the Third Street Elementary School in Los Angeles. She started off as the toughest teacher I ever had. She respected excellence and eventually, when she felt she saw it, rewarded it.

—*Mel Levine, former congressman, Los Angeles, California*

*B*ob Blackman. He was not just a great football coach at Dartmouth. He was a great teacher at an institution that has always had its share of great educators. He taught us to strive to excel—not just as individuals but also as a team, which is an indispensable lesson for life. We learned that winning comes from exhaustive preparation and an absolute commitment to excellence, not good luck or whom you know. And we learned that it is important to work smart, as well as to work hard.

—*Hank Paulson, CEO, Goldman Sachs, New York, New York*

*G*ordon Christensen, who teaches dentistry in Provo, Utah. He loves imparting the knowledge he has to others. He is practical. And he has credibility: He literally practices what he teaches.

—*Larry Peterson, dentist, Washington, D.C.*

# *I Remember* . . .

$\mathcal{M}$r. Swan, my math teacher at Taree High School in Australia. He was very patient and had a very good way with the students. It's ages ago and even though I don't remember the quadratic equation anymore I can remember the personal attention he gave every one of us.

*—Sydney Aust, customer service representative, Banff, Alberta*

$\mathcal{P}$rofessor McDowell, who taught economics at Brandon University in Manitoba. He had come from humble working roots, put himself through university but was fired with the desire to pass on knowledge. With him, economics was never a dull subject but the result of interactions between social influences, the arts, literature, and life.

*—Terry R. Colli, former foreign service officer, Brandon, Manitoba*

$\mathcal{J}$ames Dye. He was a fantastic teacher. I encountered him when I was at Michigan State. I wanted to be a scientist, but I found all the scientists really boring. But not him. He rescued me. He made me realize that science could really be alive.

*—Larry Dumas, provost, Northwestern University, Evansville, Illinois*

# *I Remember . . .*

*G*race Lawrence. She taught Western civilization at Kenmore East High School near Buffalo. She managed to get us interested in Greek and Roman history. And when she explained flying buttresses for us she made us stand up and be flying buttresses ourselves. I remember it all so vividly.

—*Susan Milligan, writer, Washington, D.C.*

*T*he best teacher I ever knew, my father. He taught mathematics at Duke. He taught me to work hard and to have discipline. But he taught by example. He took a second job at night to put us all through college. It showed me that education was worth extra effort and sacrifice. He left us no money, but he left us with that legacy.

—*David R. Gergen, aide to Presidents Nixon, Ford, Reagan, and Clinton*

*M*iss Perham. She was my fifth-grade teacher at the Horace Mann School. She sent me home because my fingernails weren't clean. They've been clean ever since.

—*Richard M. Shribman, real estate and insurance agent,*
*Salem, Massachusetts*

# *I Remember . . .*

Mrs. Kameshka, my fifth-grade teacher in West Mifflin, Pennsylvania. She got me off my behind.

—*Stan Nebinski, insurance salesman, McLean, Virginia*

Frank Longstreth. He taught Latin at Western Reserve Academy in Hudson, Ohio. I had gone to a very small public school in Ohio in a tiny town on the edge of Appalachia. I had never really been challenged academically. But this Latin course was difficult, and I wasn't doing very well. One night, right before an exam, I heard a knock on my dorm door. It was my Latin teacher, and amid all my panic, he gave me a pep talk. He told me to keep my head down and to keep at it. Things haven't always been easy for me, but I remember the time someone made the special effort for me.

—*John E. Yang, ABC News correspondent, Washington, D.C.*

*I Remember . . .*

David Grossel. He is now the deputy head of King's School, Wimbledon. I was extremely fortunate to encounter him in January 1974, when he was fresh out of university. My school suddenly found one of its history teachers had left, and he presented ideas that were at the cutting edge to high school students. He had a forensic skill that has stayed with me to the present. I still use his ideas while teaching my own students.

> —*Lawrence Goldman, historian, Oxford University, England*

Lawrence Goldman. He taught me history at Oxford. He was an Englishman and he taught me that America was a fascinating place. He was right.

> —*Gordon Corera, American political specialist,*
> *British Broadcasting Corporation, London*

Frederick Merk. He was an aging but respected teacher of the westward movement in American history. I can't remember any one thing he said. But I remember his effort to put American history in context. He made me understand why this country is a country.

> —*Michael J. Harrington, former congressman, Beverly, Massachusetts*

*M*iss Wilson, who taught the sixth grade at K. C. Lewis School in Washington. During that time the Vietnam War was raging. As children, we didn't comprehend what the war was all about. Miss Wilson put the war into perspective. We read about it, we saw it on TV, but she made us understand it.

—*Eric Jones, chauffeur, Washington, D.C.*

*P*rofessor Daniel. He told me that you should expect more from your teachers than just reading from a book. He said that college was more than a test and a book. That stuck with me. For the rest of my life, I have looked for teachers who did more.

—*David Falk, IBM regional support manager, Chicago, Illinois*

*M*iss Marks, who taught music appreciation at Madison High School. I knew absolutely nothing about classic music. Then I met her. There was darkness and then—because of her—there was light.

—*Charles Schumer, U.S. senator, Brooklyn, New York*

# *I Remember . . .*

*A* nun named Sister Pious. She knew my family and had all five of us in class. But she was always on my case. She told me I would never go anywhere. I was determined to prove her wrong. And so I worked harder for her than I ever worked before. Because of her, I became a fighter. I'm still a fighter.

—*Jean Zimdars, baker's manager, Wausau, Wisconsin*

*V*ictor Menza, who taught philosophy at Dartmouth. He was a guru, a giant. He was a supernova. He was the only brilliant person I have ever met. I took his course by accident, and it changed my life. He had all these acolytes who would hang on every word he said, and he knew it, so one day he came into class and he started in on something, and we were taking down everything, and he stopped and said: "Put your pens down. What I am saying is important."

—*Peter Mose, musician, Toronto, Ontario*

*I Remember . . .*

$\mathcal{H}$aile. He taught me math in Addis Ababa. He used to make us do all the problems we didn't want to do. And he meant so much to me that when I went back to Ethiopia I tried to find him. He had disappeared, but he did not disappear from my memory.

—*Mensur Mohamed, taxi driver, Boston, Massachusetts*

$\mathcal{M}$rs. Snead, my first-grade teacher at Kenilworth Elementary School in Washington. She kept me on my toes. She taught me that not all adults were bad people.

—*Kennice Mooney, usher, Washington, D.C.*

$\mathcal{M}$iss Valliant. She was the head of the Buckingham School for Girls. She was an old suffragist and a great character. She had standards. She had expectations for all of us. She had presence and seriousness and she took little girls absolutely seriously.

—*Ellen Goodman, syndicated columnist, Boston, Massachusetts*

Gertrude Blakeborough. She was a veteran home-economics teacher when I entered her sewing class as a high school freshman in 1968. She was an accomplished seamstress, and she guided beginners with their first stitches and advanced students through the fine techniques of tailoring. At a time when many adults were throwing up their hands in disgust with those teenage hippies, she listened and counseled countless kids. She had an ear, a heart, and a hug for teenage angst that was second to none. Her greatest skill, one I try to emulate as a teacher and parent, is the ability to be angry or frustrated with one student's behavior and then to turn around very calmly and assist another.

—*Alice Robinson, teacher, Martha's Vineyard, Massachusetts*

Professor Bill James, who taught physics at Ventura Junior College in California. He was like Mr. Wizard. He made the inexplicable understandable.

—*Jim O'Leary, program manager, Central Intelligence Agency,*
*Langley, Virginia*

# $\mathscr{I}$ Remember . . .

$\mathscr{M}$y high school math teacher at the Taft School. He kept telling us he was short but he was tough. He accomplished something tough, too: He taught a lot of high school boys that math was something they needed to succeed.

—*Phil Kimball, businessman, Washington, D.C.*

$\mathscr{M}$rs. Hill. She was my English teacher in high school in South Holland, Illinois. She opened up whole new windows for us: She taught us to view everything we read in context. I hated it. And she made us write very difficult papers. But thirty years later I am still proud of those papers. And because of her, I never settle for face value in anything.

—*Beverly DeJovine, organization development consultant, Chicago, Illinois*

$\mathscr{M}$y clarinet teacher. I remember when he told me that a musician is either great or really mediocre. He taught me that there was no in-between. So I had to be great.

—*Jeff Bieber, television producer, Columbia, Maryland*

# *I Remember . . .*

*M*iss Wright in Bremerhaven High School, which was run in post-war Germany by the Defense Department. The teachers there were young men and women who had adventure in their hearts. Miss Wright believed that you had to write every day, and at the beginning of the year she told us that unless we wrote every day we would have "literary constipation." She wanted us to have "regular habits." You can imagine how we snickered about those phrases. But we didn't get literary constipation, and we came to appreciate regular habits.

—*C. Peter Magrath, former president of the University of Missouri and the University of Minnesota, Bethesda, Maryland*

*M*rs. LeCesne, this wonderful teacher in Albuquerque, New Mexico. There weren't many black kids in Albuquerque, so to have an African-American teacher in this atmosphere of whites and Hispanics was different, to some extent exotic. She was known as a very tough teacher, and some kids were afraid to have her. By the end of the year we learned a lot of geography and the metric system—and tolerance.

—*Judy Slotnik, public relations executive, Washington, D.C.*

# *I Remember . . .*

*H*ugh McGlade. He made us call him Sir. When we misbehaved, he'd put on the West Point cadet's jacket he kept in the closet and shout "creepy kids" at us. He played show tunes on a portable turntable while we worked. He made us memorize Shakespeare and Kipling. He believed that a bunch of lower-middle-class fifth-graders in a Long Island public school could benefit from a classical education. And Sir was correct.

—*Dana Milbank, writer, Washington, D.C.*

*H*ans Schadler. He's now the chef at Caneel Bay in the Virgin Islands. He taught me how to cook and how to deal with people, but he also taught me that a sense of taste was most of all an awakening.

—*Mike Gray, executive chef, the Hanover Inn, Hanover, New Hampshire*

*M*iss Gray. She taught first grade in North Quincy, Massachusetts I remember her with graying hair, wearing gray, and looking gray. But I remember one other thing: She taught me how to read.

—*Chris Rath, superintendent of schools, Concord, New Hampshire*

# I Remember . . .

Mrs. Armentrut, my English teacher in high school. She instilled in us the idea that no matter how people want to analyze literature, it is basically art. She taught us to read for the sheer pleasure of it, and even when I am reading something like *Scientific American* I do it for the pleasure of it.

—*Steve Johnson, director of sales for a commercial-spacecraft company*

Mrs. Sinclair, my first-grade teacher. My brother and I were the only Catholic kids in a very small, totally Protestant upstate New York town. Every day we recited the Lord's Prayer. At that time the Catholic version of the Lord's Prayer was shorter than the Protestant version. I would always end my version a few seconds earlier than the rest of the class. I knew that I was different. But one day Mrs. Sinclair, knowing that all the other kids were at after-school activities at their respective Protestant churches, took us by the hand and walked us to the Methodist church and announced to those in charge that we had been left out and asked if we could play with the other children. This teacher's simple act of kindness taught us a lot.

—*Kathleen P. Iannello, associate professor of political science,*
*Gettysburg College, Gettysburg, Pennsylvania*

# *I Remember . . .*

*M*iss Taintor, my fourth-grade teacher at Hindley School in Darien, Connecticut. I was interested in everything she taught: dinosaurs, conservation, and art. I thought she was ten feet tall and looked like Abraham Lincoln. She was that big to me.

—*Reeve Lindbergh, daughter of the aviator, Vermont*

*M*r. Olson. He was my social studies and English teacher in the seventh and eighth grades. He was a man who was passionate about learning. He would play classical music and make us talk about it. He would lead us in endless discussions about poetry. He was a paragon of the virtues of learning. He towered over my life, and he does even now.

—*Robert W. Merry, publisher,* Congressional Quarterly, McLean, Virginia

*M*rs. Barber. She was my third-grade teacher in Hollywood, Florida, the year my father died. She was young and soft and gentle, and she got me through a very hard time.

—*Tamora Farmer, dental hygienist, Washington, D.C.*

# $\mathcal{I}$ $\mathcal{R}emember$ . . .

$\mathcal{J}$ohn W. Miller, who taught me philosophy at Williams College. He was so much admired by the students that he always had enormous classes. And he set the class at eight A.M. hoping to shrink the crowd. I promised myself as an undergraduate that I would dedicate my first book to him but I was too slow. He died before I could finish it.

—*Noel Perrin, adjunct professor of environmental studies, Dartmouth College, Hanover, New Hampshire*

$\mathcal{J}$oel Schwartz, who taught at the University of North Carolina. Quite often college professors aren't good teachers. But he wasn't a good teacher; he was a great teacher—so good that he inspired me to be a teacher.

—*Paul Wellstone, U.S. senator and former college professor, St. Paul, Minnesota*

*M*iss Harrod. She was my English teacher in high school. She was the most demanding and most disapproving teacher I ever had. She made us write every day and then she tore up everything I wrote. But then something snapped—and she accepted me. She was just as demanding but she didn't make me feel stupid anymore.

—*Margo Bode, Evanston, Illinois*

*M*rs. Hawkes. She was my third-grade teacher in Scituate, Rhode Island She was like her name: a hawk lady. She loved birds. She inspired me to enjoy learning. She even made the hard things fun. It was so much fun that we didn't even realize we were learning things.

—*Robert N. Liptrot, engineer, Boxford, Massachusetts*

*J*oseph Prusan. He taught eleventh-grade American history in Cheltenham High School just north of Philadelphia. He had a real ability to teach the subject in a way that was exciting but also complex. He broadened me.

—*Bruce Freed, Washington, D.C.*

# I Remember . . .

Jack Barnaby, my squash coach at Harvard. I was the ninth player on the team—which is one way of saying that I was the worst player on the team. One day we were playing Navy and I was in the deciding match against a very tough opponent. I said to Jack that my opponent was too tough, that I couldn't compete against him. And he told me that I could beat him. It turned out that I did win. I learned a lesson that day—that if you believed, you could succeed.

—*Stephen Sonnabend, businessman, Key Biscayne, Florida*

Pete Carril. He was my high school basketball coach in Reading, Pennsylvania, long before he went to Princeton and became famous, and I sat in his Problems of Democracy class during the Cuban Missile Crisis. We had a quiz every day in his class. He had a passion for what he did. He was a role model. He was tremendously exacting and discerning. He had a presence and he instilled fear. Everyone knew his expectations—and he inspired us to achieve our potential.

—*Gary Walters, athletic director, Princeton University, Princeton, New Jersey*

# *I Remember . . .*

$\mathscr{M}$rs. Adler, who was my English teacher in the eleventh grade. She had an incredible passion for poetry and literature. My class was just in her thrall. And when she showed me the recommendation she wrote for me for college, I was astonished. She really, really noticed me.

—*Jill Zuckman, congressional correspondent,* Chicago Tribune, *Washington, D.C.*

$\mathscr{M}$rs. Eldredge, my first-grade teacher in Freedom, New Hampshire. I was very shy, but she was caring and gave us a lot of attention, and the more I teach the more I think kids need that—to be cared for, to be given attention, to be acknowledged and respected as a person even though they are little outside.

—*Connie Griffin, teacher, Hudson, Massachusetts*

$\mathscr{S}$hannon Webster, my English teacher in eleventh grade in Littleton, Massachusetts. I was bright but very shy. But she always had time for us. She nurtured every one of her pupils. And she got me to go out for the school play. I've been a show-off ever since.

—*Judy Swallow, BBC news anchor, London*

# ℐ Remember . . .

ℳr. Snow. He taught me politics and social affairs at Sea Pines School for Girls in East Brewster, Massachusetts. I had never been all that interested in politics. He made me aware of how politics affected our daily lives, and he taught that people could actually make a difference if they got involved. I've lived by that since.

—*Karin Marks, city counselor, Westmount, Quebec*

ℳy high-school English teacher in Tyler, Texas. More than fifty years later, after I was speaking somewhere, a woman came up to me and asked if I had been schooled by Sarah Marsh. She was a small and elegant woman. She never raised her voice. But we were terrified of her. She had such high standards that she pulled out of us the very best we had in us. We wanted desperately to do our work well. She taught me, even at fifteen, the difference between a punk performance and a good one.

—*Harry C. McPherson, lawyer and Lyndon Johnson aide,*
*Washington, D.C.*

𝒟r. Regis L. Boyle, who taught high school journalism in Maryland. She was an incredible professional, exacting and determined. She treated the high school paper as if it were a real paper. I learned a lot from her that I carry to this day. Her mantra was: accuracy and reliability. It's my mantra now.

—*Richard L. Berke, chief political writer,* The New York Times, *Washington, D.C.*

𝒨r. Loranger, who was one of my teachers in the seventh grade in Manchester, New Hampshire. He was what you would call a hippie. All the other teachers were clean-cut, but he had long hair, and it was always messy. But he showed everyone that even though he looked different he could be the same.

—*Diane Vlahos, secretary, Concord, New Hampshire*

𝒨rs. Feever. She was my high school English teacher. I used to believe that people who hadn't had a personal tragedy were ripe to get one. But she told me that it was unlikely that there would be any tragedy in my entire life. She righted me, and she was right.

—*Cathy Supple, San Marcos, Texas*

# *I Remember . . .*

Mrs. Barnes, who was my first-grade teacher. I was terrified of going to school. She calmed me down. I'm forty-four now, and I still remember how scared I was—and how she reassured me.

—*Mary Mothersole, medical receptionist, Washington, D.C.*

Captain Max Buck, who taught Latin and German at the Western Military Academy in Alton, Illinois, and who is responsible for everything I know about grammar. But one day I was reading aloud one of those German sentences that end with seventeen verbs, and Captain Buck said: "Mr. Vanocur, if you ever have a chance to do something with your voice, do it."

—*Sandy Vanocur, retired NBC News broadcaster,*
*Santa Barbara, California*

Guy Lentini, who was my math teacher at South Boston High. I was kind of a wise guy in school, and every time I wised off he kept me after school. He gave me the discipline I didn't have.

—*J. Joseph Moakley, late congressman, Boston, Massachusetts*

# I Remember . . .

$\mathcal{J}$. Prescott Johnson, who taught me philosophy at Bethany Nazarene College. He introduced me to the world of ideas and made me think in a structural way. He made me understand life wasn't a struggle between the soul and the mind. It was both.

—*Gary W. Hart, former senator, Denver, Colorado*

$\mathcal{B}$ob Shapiro, who was my social studies teacher in Pilgrim High School in Warwick, Rhode Island. He inspired me to think about public affairs and current events. He organized a model legislature. The thing about him was that he cared, and he cared about whether we thought or not.

—*Walter S. Mossberg, computer columnist,* The Wall Street Journal, *Washington, D.C.*

$\mathcal{B}$ill Stanley, the band director at Hall High in West Hartford, Connecticut. He had very high standards and he brought us up to those standards. He refused to be dragged down to ours.

—*David Sachs, clinical psychologist and trombonist, Washington, D.C.*

# *I Remember . . .*

*B*ob Williams. He was an art teacher at Georgetown College in Kentucky. He would challenge us to draw, and I would work on these beautiful pictures and he would come over and sneer: "Make some art." I struggled to do it. I moved into the art building. I worked nonstop. I tried everything and reached as much as I could and finally he looked at one of my pictures and said: "This is art."

—*Reverend James Somerville, pastor of First Baptist Church, Washington, D.C.*

*M*iss Huiting, my eighth-grade teacher. She was the only teacher who made us read whole huge chunks of text. If you made any noise in class, she'd put you in a closet. But she so obviously cared that if you tried as hard as she did, she prized you—and followed your career for years.

—*Michael Finnerty, radio producer, London, Ontario*

*D*r. Billingsley, one of my professors at Virginia Tech. He taught finance—and inspired me. He had confidence in our futures.

—*Carol Catalano, pharmaceutical representative, Clifton, Virginia*

$\mathscr{C}$hristine Dethier, my violin teacher. She didn't make me love music, she showed me how much I did love music. And it wasn't that she made me think she was a big deal. It was that she made me think Mozart and Bach were big deals.

—*Nina Falk, violinist, Takoma Park, Maryland*

$\mathscr{E}$phraim Stam, my nuclear-engineering professor at North Carolina State University. He was one of those teachers whose students lived in complete terror of him. There was one formula for a nuclear reaction that he told us we had to remember, just absolutely had to know, even if he called us up at three in the morning. I was thirty-six years old when my daughter was born and, in labor, was able to recite the four-factor formula.

—*Suzanne Phelps, nuclear engineer, Washington, D.C.*

$\mathscr{M}$r. Laraway. He was my teacher in sixth grade. He was a very challenging teacher. We read "Lady of the Lake" that year, and we were in way over our heads. But we all felt very accomplished once we finished it. He taught me to take on a challenge.

—*Mary Wallack, stockbroker, Washington, D.C.*

# *I Remember . . .*

*P*enny Gill, who taught me at Mount Holyoke. I had gone to a very progressive high school before Mount Holyoke, which I found very traditional. I wanted to leave the place. But she told me, in more ways than one, that I could do anything I wanted. She gave me permission to use my creativity and passion.

—*Kathleen Hirsch, writer, Boston, Massachusetts*

*G*ordon Hamilton, my eighth-grade teacher in Schenectady, New York. I'm forty-nine now, I'm still in school, and I still haven't had another teacher care about me as much as he did.

—*Laura Skinner Davis, physical-therapy student, Arlington, Virginia*

*B*rother Amian Paul, my English teacher at LaSalle Academy in Providence. He had an intimidating manner. He shook me into realizing I had academic potential. He did that literally by shaking me.

—*Jack Reed, U.S. senator, Cranston, Rhode Island*

# $\mathcal{I}\,\mathcal{R}emember\ldots$

$\mathcal{M}$rs. Washington, my basketball coach. She was fair, she played everybody equally, and she didn't only coach us in basketball. She coached us about life.

—*Deva Tucker, lifeguard, Falls Church, Virginia*

$\mathcal{D}$r. Deill, my music teacher at Garden City High School in New York. He taught a complicated system of music, but he treated us as adults, he gave us responsibility, and he helped us deal with responsibility.

—*Robert Stevenson, congressional aide, Washington, D.C.*

$\mathcal{M}$r. Cornet, my chemistry and trigonometry teacher at Robinson High School in Fairfax, Virginia. He won our respect because he had a lot of respect for us.

—*Lisa Oberegon, homemaker, Springfield, Virginia*

# I Remember . . .

Sandy Schneider, who taught me English literature at the University of Iowa. She made it all fun and exciting. She painted a picture of each book for us. I can still see those pictures.

—*Wendy Sutton, homemaker, Centreville, Virginia*

Joan Assey, my tenth-grade English teacher. She taught me that organization was everything.

—*April Oliver, television producer, Washington, D.C.*

Dr. Bonelli. He teaches the current-events course I take with some other senior citizens in Westchester. Most of us have forgotten a lot of history, but he reminds us that current events started way back. He taught a lot of us older people that there is nothing much new.

—*Rosalind Schulkin, retired medical administrator,*
*New Rochelle, New York*

# I Remember . . .

Peter Leonhardt, my swim coach when I was thirteen. He made us learn to love the sport and he made the learning process fun. I had fifty swim coaches in my life, but he is the one I try to emulate. I try to be as gentle as he was.

—*Danielle Frottier, swim coach, Washington, D.C.*

Mrs. Finn, my wonderful high school classics and ancient-history teacher. She made writers dead for thousands of years come alive every afternoon.

—*Emily Mulvoy, marketing executive, New York, New York*

Gene Rizer. He was one of my math teachers at Falls Church High School. He knew how to relate to people like me who hate math.

—*Bill Shirley, gymnastics instructor, Annandale, Virginia*

Coach Gleeson. He was my basketball coach. He made us all feel like we were winning even when we were losing.

—*Jason Shirley, manager of a recreation center, Virginia*

# *I Remember* . . .

*M*s. Johnson, the director of the Modern School in Harlem. She could be a terrifying figure—she hid a Ping-Pong paddle in her office—but she saturated us with care and pride. At fifty-eight, I realize that my seven years with her seasoned my values.

—*Stanford A. Roman Jr., dean, Sophie Davis School of Biomedical Education/CUNY Medical School, New York, New York*

*P*rofessor David Wiggins. He was my adviser at George Mason University. I had him in his "Sports History" class, and he picked up on my interest. He connected with me.

—*Geordie Bigus, elementary physical-education teacher, Oakton, Virginia*

*S*ister Loretta Frances, my first-grade teacher. School could have been hard, but she made it easy.

—*Linda McGill, claims examiner, Annandale, Virginia*

# *I Remember . . .*

$\mathcal{M}$rs. Mamie Bacote, who was one of my high school teachers in Newport News, Virginia. She always taught students to "reach beyond" our day-to-day lives. She stopped me in the hallway one day in my senior year and told me she knew just what college I should attend. She mentioned Dartmouth College. I had never heard of it. And I had no interest in anyplace in New Hampshire; surely there were no black people in New Hampshire. She bugged me and bugged me about it, and finally I applied, just to get her off my back.

—*Nelson Armstrong, director of alumni relations, Dartmouth College, Hanover, New Hampshire*

$\mathcal{M}$r. Hudspeth, my freshman English teacher who taught us how to read a work of fiction. He seemed almost too big for the drafty, pre-fab classroom on the edge of campus where we met a couple of times a week. But he neither intimidated nor dominated. He taught us instead how to pay attention. We learned to tease meaning from myth, insight from image.

—*Evelynne Kramer, editor, Brookline, Massachusetts*

# *I Remember . . .*

*M*rs. Baxter, my English teacher at East High School. I still write to her. She sends me birthday cards, anniversary cards, Christmas cards. I always know she cares.

—*Jean Davidson, Anchorage, Alaska*

*R*abbi Cashten. He taught the philosophy course I took at Bowie State. I never met a rabbi before, and I didn't know much about Judaism, but he taught me how to think.

—*Richard Carter, home-heating-oil executive, Marlboro, Maryland*

*C*oleman Karesh, who taught law at the University of South Carolina. He knew so much about trusts and torts that we thought the citations that were in our books were in Braille on his behind.

—*Ernest F. Hollings, U.S. senator, Charleston, South Carolina*

*J*ames Cox. Toward the end of my junior year at Dartmouth, I stopped by his office unannounced and I told him I wanted to work with him on a senior thesis about Mark Twain. Twain was his specialty. "I don't want to work on Twain," he said. "How about Hawthorne?" He forced me to read in a different light. There were moments when he'd be rambling, and I would be overwhelmed by a new set of implications he gave to something very ordinary. My meetings with him turned into a series of moments you sometimes have in the presence of somebody who helps you see in ways you never saw before. When I was with Cox, time seemed to stop.

—*Susan G. Dentzer, correspondent,* The NewsHour with Jim Lehrer, *Shirlington, Virginia*

*M*adeleine Sullivan, my seventh-grade teacher at P.S. 120 in Flushing, Queens. She was small and chubby but she took no guff. And I was a typical seventh-grader. One day I talked back to her. She wheeled around and, jumping in the air, slapped me. I was stunned, but I have been grateful to her ever since.

—*Jose Cabranes, federal circuit judge, New Haven, Connecticut*

# *I Remember . . .*

Frank Jeffers, my high school social studies teacher at West Morris Regional High School in Chester, New Jersey. He made me see the importance of keeping up with what was going on in this world. To this day I can still remember him coming into class the morning after the Cuban Missile Crisis barely able to teach, he was so upset and so nervous. He was that afraid for all of us.

—*Terry Dalton, professor, Western Maryland College,*
*Westminster, Maryland*

Joe Sikora, whom I had in both seventh and eighth grades in Woodbine, New Jersey. I need a lot of motivation. He was the best motivator I ever saw.

—*Ro Lesiw, attorney, Postal Workers Union, Washington, D.C.*

Mr. Bukowski, my math teacher in high school. In senior year he let us teach his class. We saw how hard teaching was, and how special he was.

—*Ron Keech, pharmacist, Bethesda, Maryland*

# ℐ Remember . . .

𝒜rchibald L. Hepworth. The name sounded so dry, so starchy, yet the man was anything but. He made eleventh-grade American history at Williston Northampton School come alive, instilled in me a lifelong passion for history, and taught me a valuable lesson in the geometry of critical thought: that all issues have more than one side.

*—Steve Robbins, benefits manager, Hartford, Connecticut*

𝒢race Moore, my sophomore English teacher. Her classroom had a magnificent view of Nahant Bay, and I spent most of each class looking out the window. But she was the first teacher who ever told me of my great potential and talent. I was too young to realize what a gift she was in my life.

*—Mary E. B. Kiley, manager of building operations, New England Conservatory of Music, Boston, Massachusetts*

𝒥im Flanagan. He was my first real swim coach. He taught me more than how to swim laps and yards. He taught me the mental and passionate side of swimming.

*—Ted Pierson, swim coach, Washington, D.C.*

# *I Remember . . .*

*K*enneth Scollin, my art teacher at White Oak Junior High. He didn't only teach us art, though. He also taught us about world history, and he did it through art. I never would have paid any attention to the Romans in history class, but I did in art class.

—*Johanne Danver, YMCA aquatic assistant,*
*Montgomery Village, Maryland*

*C*harles S. Hyneman, one of my government professors at Indiana University in the 1960s. In each of the two classes I took from him, the only requirement was a paper. But through the sheer force of his personality and teaching style, I came to believe that the Hyneman paper was the overriding academic obligation of the semester, not so much for the research he required as for the depth of thought. I may not remember specific topics from his class, but I hope I remember how to think.

—*Craig Klugman, editor,* Fort Wayne Journal Gazette,
*Fort Wayne, Indiana*

# *I Remember* . . .

*C*harles Alan Wright, my constitutional law professor at the University of Texas. He was one of the most outstanding legal minds of our time. He would talk and I would sop it up.

*—Kay Bailey Hutchison, U.S. senator, Dallas, Texas*

*G*erry Bernstein, an art historian at Brandeis University. He taught me about the intersection of light and space and the juxtaposition of buildings to their surroundings. But he also taught me about history and society. He allowed me to make the connection between my two loves—history and art—with one simple phrase: Art is merely a reflection of the socioeconomic climate of the times. That phrase has stuck with me to this day.

*—Hillel J. Korin, associate vice president, Brandeis University, Waltham, Massachusetts*

*M*onique Mercure, who was my grade two teacher at Ecole St. Michel in Brossard, Quebec. We learned a lot and there was no pain to it at all. For all the other teachers there was real pain.

*—Louise Richer, accountant, Montreal, Quebec*

Thomas H. O'Connor. He taught basic American history at Boston College in the late 1950s, but he specialized in the middle period, as it was called: the time between the revolution and the Civil War. He was proof that there is no dull period in history—and he was a great mimic. He brought Calhoun, Webster, Van Buren, Clay all to life. He taught me that history is not a dull and dusty thing, but full of life and rich in humor—like Thomas O'Connor himself.

—*Martin F. Nolan, writer, San Francisco, California*

Professor Thomas Stritch. He taught "American Culture" at Notre Dame in a state of rebellious dissent. Like an umpire who's not always right yet never in doubt, he asserted his views with challenging gusto. I rarely agreed with what he said—and only later learned the larger lesson of his teaching art. He forced undergraduates to think for themselves—for the first time.

—*Robert P. Schmuhl, professor of American studies,*
*University of Notre Dame, South Bend, Indiana*

$\mathcal{P}$aula Baron, my high school history teacher. She made us work when most of the teachers didn't make us do anything. She didn't let us slack off.

—*Julie Abrams, business consultant, Bethesda, Maryland*

$\mathcal{P}$rofessor Ettinger. She taught at the Radcliffe Seminars at Harvard. And listening to this woman discuss literature, even books you have read before, was like opening an entirely new book that shined. *Dr. Zhivago* by yourself is one thing. *Dr. Zhivago* with her was something entirely different.

—*Thaleia Schlesinger, communications consultant,*
*Brookline, Massachusetts*

$\mathcal{M}$y senior year in college, I was the teaching assistant in a class and I told the professor I had to go on a job interview. And he said to me: "Why are you going on a job interview when you should be going to graduate school?" Until that moment—that very second—it had never occurred to me that I was smart enough to do that.

—*Patrice Franko, economist, Waterville, Maine*

# *I Remember . . .*

$\mathscr{M}$r. Merlo, who began my seventh-grade science class with a preview of the year. "And in January," he said with a mischievous gleam in his eye, "chapter five—Fires!" He rubbed his hands diabolically, and we loved him instantly. He showed us how to create an exploding ball of flame by blowing cornstarch from a paper cone across a Bunsen burner. He tried to make water by combing hydrogen and oxygen in a cardboard milk carton, then applied a burning flame to the mouth. After many failures, he continued the experiment after school in his basement classroom for those of us brave enough to hang around. Finally, ka-BOOM. As he crawled around the floor picking up bits of cardboard to show us the drops of water, the rotund janitor ran past the door, yelling, "The boiler's exploded, the boiler's exploded." Mr. Merlo was not there the next year.

—*David K. Shipler, writer, Chevy Chase, Maryland*

$\mathscr{M}$ademoiselle Powell, my high school French teacher. She demonstrated the difference between *en* and *dans* by jumping into the wastebasket and getting stuck there.

—*Joan A. Osborne, teacher, Derby, N.Y.*

# ℐ Remember . . .

𝒴ves Rouillard, my grade eight geography teacher at Bialik High School in Montreal. He had a great character. He loved what he did. He was the first person who was able to take all the vague notions I had about life and help me organize them. I went back to the school years later and bumped into him in the halls. I told him how much he had meant to me. His hair was almost all gray, and I asked him why it had changed. He ran his fingers through the hair and he said: "One whole side is from you."

—*Dan Dunsky, senior producer at TVOntario, Toronto, Ontario*

𝒻ather Shakespeare Rowan. He taught English lit at Loras College in Dubuque, Iowa. He introduced me to the classics. I had never heard of the classics. We called him "Shakes," and he had a little problem with the sauce, and sometimes we would ask him why his nose was so red. He would say that it was blushing with pride because it kept itself out of other people's business.

—*John Reilly, lawyer, Washington, D.C.*

# *I Remember . . .*

$\mathcal{M}$artin Noregaard, who taught seventh- and eighth-grade English and history at Brooklyn Friends School in New York. He combined a real academic rigor with compassion and humor. That made him really inspiring—but really demanding in the best senses of that word.

*—Stephen J. Wermiel, professor of constitutional law,*
*American University, Washington, D.C.*

$\mathcal{P}$aul Connolly, a teaching assistant in my freshman year in college. He taught literature to students who did not give a hoot about the great novels he tried to pack into our lummoxy heads. But he retained a verve and love for what he was doing that won many of us over in time. Using good cheer, patience, and rigorous standards he demonstrated how those who succeed in writing wrapped themselves up in honesty, compassion, uncompromising dedication to message and language. His lessons were simple: Never cut corners, never forget who you are, and never set out without knowing your goal. He was a good soul.

*—Denis Horgan, writer, Hartford, Connecticut*

$\mathcal{B}$yron Nichols, a new recruit in the political-science department at Union College. He was fresh out of grad school; I was a college student who had all the answers. We made a deal: I taught him about our chaotic campus culture in the late 1960s, he taught me about the disciplined conduct of inquiry. I got the better bargain because his rigid application of the scientific method in social research gave me the tools to look for answers before trying to change things.

—*Jeffrey C. Browne, public-relations executive, Milwaukee, Wisconsin*

$\mathcal{M}$argaret Staats, my seventh- and eighth-grade English teacher. She wrote a comment in the margin of one of my seventh-grade compositions that still resonates and instructs. I'd handed in a scathing essay about my grandfather's funeral and the adult hypocrisy I thought surrounded it. Ms. Staats said I needed to develop a "more sympathetic imagination." I was bewildered. The essay was nonfiction, and I wondered how imagination could be an issue. She sent me to the dictionary, where one definition of imagination was "the ability to deal creatively with reality." Ever since, I've kept my sympathetic imagination and my dictionary close by when I write.

—*Rachel Gorlin, writer, Washington, D.C.*

# I Remember . . .

Minnie Lloyd, who taught me at Short Ridge High School in Indianapolis. She was the person the school used to introduce us to the SAT, which was not widely taken in 1947. She coached us for hours, right from the beginning of our freshman year. The idea was to get us into selective colleges. She gave us a comprehensive worldview, but she also taught us to set goals.

—*Richard Lugar, U.S. senator, Indianapolis, Indiana*

Mr. Morrison. This goes back to junior high school, and he was a health instructor. He was so interesting because he was a highly disciplined individual. You looked at him and thought Marine Corps. But he was so good at taking young minds and training them and filling them with important stuff.

—*Steve Logue, manager, Canaan Valley State Park,*
*Canaan Valley, West Virginia*

Robert Prevost, my math teacher in La Beauce St. Georges, Quebec. He was funny. He taught technical stuff with jokes. It was a great way to teach.

—*Jessica Poulin, bookseller, Lake Louise, Alberta*

# *I Remember* . . .

*M*iss Walker, my first-grade teacher at Davy Crockett Elementary School in Houston. I didn't come from a bookish family, but because she read so much to us, I came to relish reading, and I've been doing it for seventy years. It was the most important thing I learned ever.

—*Jack Valenti, president, Motion Picture Association of America,*
*Washington, D.C.*

*A*lexander M. Bickel, the great constitutional-law scholar at Yale and a student and protégé of Felix Frankfurter. He had a theory of the law that was breathtaking in its capacity to explain a vast expanse of legal activity. A whole generation of law students worshiped him.

—*James O. Freedman, former president, Dartmouth College,*
*Hanover, New Hampshire*

*D*ebbie Cooper, who taught travel and tourism. She knew the travel industry inside and out. She's the reason I sit all day at an airport in Toronto.

—*Diana Falcone, gate agent, Toronto, Ontario*

# *I Remember . . .*

John Kemeny, who taught me calculus as a college freshman. Professor Kemeny had an extraordinary ability to understand students' questions even when they weren't able to articulate those questions in a comprehensible way. As a teacher, I have learned how important it is to listen to my students as a way of becoming a better teacher.

—*Robert M. Saltzman, associate dean,*
*University of Southern California Law School, Los Angeles, California*

Miss Isabelle Pease. She taught English at Deering High School in Portland, Maine. She thought I should be a writer. She took some of the kids who cared about writing and she sent us out to interview people. I loved it and loved her.

—*Donald R. Larrabee, writer, Bethesda, Maryland*

Mrs. Washington. She was my eighth-grade teacher at O. Henry Junior High School in Austin. She scared the tar out of us, so we really paid attention. She had us do experiments outside. She made us experience science—and life.

—*Rebecca Lack, secretary, Austin, Texas*

# *I Remember . . .*

*S*ister Michael Agnes. She was my first-grade teacher in Gardner, Massachusetts, and even at a young age I understood that her entire life revolved around the six rows of seven kids in our class. Those forty-two kids were everything for her.

—*Mark D. Gearan, president, Hobart and William Smith Colleges,*
*Geneva, New York*

*E*dward Meagher, who taught English my first two years of high school. He assigned a composition every week. One day in my freshman year, he read my composition aloud with great energy. "This was not written by a senior," he said. "This was written by someone in your own class."

—*David W. Johnson, writer and teacher, Emory and Henry College,*
*Emory, Virginia*

*M*r. Panzer, who taught me in grade twelve in Weston Collegiate High School. He invited us over for barbecue. He was funny. He cared. He was a teacher, but he knew how to be one of the kids.

—*Vierna Stamatis, Air Canada representative, Toronto, Ontario*

# *I Remember . . .*

*C*ecelia Brinton, the psychologist at the Buckingham School in Cambridge, Massachusetts. She was also my grandmother, and her experience in a neurological clinic in Boston gave her the training to recognize that I was dyslexic long before dyslexia was generally recognized. In 1951, this was a very lucky thing for me indeed. That fall of first grade was a turning point for me; all of my classmates rocketed ahead with the discovery of the power of reading while I just couldn't seem to figure out the secret of it. My grandmother recognized that my problem was not stupidity or organic damage.

—*Jock Gill, businessman, Boston, Massachusetts*

*M*r. Harder. He was a shop teacher with a big neck. He was so tough and imposed such standards. He taught me skills, like how to build a corner shelf, but he taught me discipline. My mother and father worked all day in the store, and if I was irascible the most they could do was crack me upside the head. They didn't have time to talk to me about discipline. But Mr. Harder did.

—*Mario M. Cuomo, former governor of New York*

$\mathcal{M}$iss Louise Bowman. She was the fifth-grade teacher at Arab Elementary in Arab, Alabama. For one of her projects she asked us all to pick our favorite American. I chose Senator Joseph McCarthy. I was a kid in Alabama and I was doing what everybody in Alabama told me to do: hate Communists. Well, she made me, at age eleven, read *The Gulag Archipelago.* She actually bought it and gave it to me. And for three months I read the book on the school bus my grandfather drove. When I read the whole damn thing she told me that tyranny of any sort was bad and that ordinary people can get hurt when ideologies go crazy. Good lesson.

—*Rodney Ferguson, public-relations executive, Washington, D.C.*

$\mathcal{E}$verett Rees. He was my English teacher in my senior year at Shawnee Mission East High School. I tried to give an oral book report to him on a book I hadn't read. He asked me questions, my answers made no sense, and he knew it. He told me to read the book and come back. I did, and I learned that it is easier to do the work than to fake it. Better, too.

—*Lisa Tarry, editor, Prairie Village, Kansas*

# *I Remember...*

*P*rofessor Nowak, who taught me history at Boston University. He was a great scholar, a great lecturer, and a great discussion leader. I took everything he taught. I learned about the Renaissance, the Balkans, and Russia. These were courses so terrific that I never even thought of cutting them. He made mere words meaningful.

—*Charles F. Kimball, retired principal, South Hadley High School, South Hadley, Massachusetts*

*M*rs. Stoll, my sixth-grade teacher at Forestdale School in Rumson, New Jersey. I came home from the first day of school in tears because the teacher was so mean. She was strict and she was stern, but she set out the ground rules, and they were harsh. And then she turned out to be the warmest and best teacher I ever had.

—*Vicki Barker, anchor,* World Update *radio program, London*

*M*r. Slater, who taught art at Great Snakey High School in Liverpool. He was very young, very outgoing, and he encouraged the students. I never became an art teacher but I still enjoy art.

—*Cindy Riggle, staff assistant, Liverpool, England*

# *I Remember . . .*

*J.* Bard McNulty, who taught me English at Trinity College in Hartford in my sophomore year. He thought he noticed some potential in me. I was an economics major, planning a career in business, but I could spell and write a complete sentence. He convinced me I should perfect my writing skills. That advice defined my life. Now I'm either a businessman who can write or a writer with business instincts. I'm not sure which.

—*Richard Hirsch, writer and public-relations consultant,*
*Buffalo, New York*

*M*ichael Rubin, who taught English at Woodlands High School in Hartsdale, New York. He was a published novelist who ended up teaching creative writing at Stanford. But for those of us in high school, he was a revelation. He exposed us to a scope of literature that was unimaginable. I had a lot of teachers who were bright people. But I only had one who didn't want his own views parroted back to him. He was an original, and he wanted us to be original.

—*James Isaacs, music commentator, Brookline, Massachusetts*

# ℐ Remember . . .

𝒮ondra Nance, my teacher at Hyer Elementary School in Dallas. I learned so much. She was so patient. She taught me everyday skills, like how to deal with people and how to be independent. I learned those things in the fifth grade.

*—Tami Kimes, sales representative, Austin, Texas*

𝐵ud Orne, who coached me and hundreds of others in our town in hockey. He showed me how to care about other people and he taught me not to give up, ever. That's a big part of my life today, and I didn't get it in any class. I got it in hockey, and I got it from Bud.

*—Jonathan Richmond, businessman, Marblehead, Massachusetts*

𝑀r. Ward, who taught history at Walt Whitman High School in Bethesda, Maryland. He'd go off and just talk—talk about this, about that, about everything. We listened to him because he always had passion and always had something to say.

*—Dana Berg, cashier, Bethesda, Maryland*

$\mathscr{M}$rs. Balk, a brand-new young teacher from Minnesota, which to us in New Haven seemed like a million miles away. I was in the third grade, and here was a teacher that had us bake bread and churn butter and do projects. She had a ton of energy and I loved the experience of merely being in the same room with her.

*—Ande Zellman, editor, Boston, Massachusetts*

$\mathscr{R}$obert Nault, my grade eight teacher in Oxdrift Public School in Ontario. We had lots of class work and lots of field trips. He got me ready for high school. In those days, that was a big achievement.

*—Herman Vogel, pool attendant, Banff, Alberta*

$\mathscr{M}$rs. Prunier, who taught art at Nashua High School in New Hampshire. But though she taught art, she was really a counselor. She was open. You could talk to her. She didn't have time to be bitter about the system because she spent all her time caring about the students.

*—Harriett Knoll, optician, Bethesda, Maryland*

J. Frank Dobie. He was a writer and a collector of stories about Texas. He was a great character, strutting up and down the class-room at the University of Texas, and he enticed you into learning, and believing, the folklore of Texas. He taught us to be story-tellers—he believed storytelling was an art form—and a lot of us became just that.

—*Liz Carpenter, former White House aide, Austin, Texas*

Miss O'Toole, who was my fourth-grade teacher in Tonawanda, New York. My dad was in the Navy and he was always gone on those month-long cruises. She had a military dad, too, and she understood. She had a lot of patience with me.

—*Jason Kmet, manager of guest services, Washington Capitals hockey team, Washington, D.C.*

Ginny Koss, who taught American history at Stone Ridge High School in Bethesda, Maryland. She had us debate. She made us play roles. She really taught us more than history: how to love history.

—*Shawn K. Feddeman, deputy press secretary, governor's office, Boston, Massachusetts*

# $\mathcal{I}\,\mathcal{R}emember\ldots$

$\mathcal{M}$r. Williams, my high school science teacher. He loved to teach us how to mix chemicals, and one day he told me that if you mixed two chemicals—I still remember which ones—you could create the world's best stink bomb. So I went to the drugstore and bought the stuff and went up to the third floor and mixed them up, just as he told me to. And within minutes they had to close down the whole school. I never told anyone that I did it, but Mr. Williams knew.

—*Henry Champ, Brandon, Manitoba*

$\mathcal{D}$eWitt Reddick. I had a degree in history and philosophy at the University of Texas, but I realized I had to have a profession. So I enrolled in the journalism program and encountered Professor Reddick. I felt I couldn't wait to get to his class.

—*Lady Bird Johnson, West Lake Hills, Texas*

$\mathcal{G}$eorge Peterson, my grade six teacher in Red Deer, Alberta. He was fun and creative. He also let us play floor hockey in class.

—*Gerry Winchester, marketing consultant, Edmonton, Alberta*

# *I Remember . . .*

$\mathcal{M}$r. Fitzgerald. He was my social studies teacher in seventh grade. I was one of only three black kids at South Hadley Intermediate School, but that was back in the days I thought I could do anything. He made me think that.

—*Christina McHenry, senior producer,* Washington Week in Review, *Shirlington, Virginia*

$\mathcal{N}$ancy Blankenship, who was my junior high school English teacher. She forced me to learn to write. And if I hadn't had her, I would never have survived philosophy and political science in college. And because of her, I double-majored in those subjects.

—*Andrea McDaniel, outreach coordinator, the Brookings Institution, Washington, D.C.*

$\mathcal{M}$rs. Green. She was an English teacher in my third year of secondary school. I'm from a French family in Quebec. She performed a miracle. She made me appreciate English.

—*Marie-Eve Michaud, concierge, St. Pamphile, Quebec*

*F*red Soltow, the head coach of the Canaan Timberline Ski Team. He was funny. He knew the game. He brought me from a little snowplower to a Junior Olympian. That was a big leap.

—*Chris Cooper, lawyer, Parsons, West Virginia*

*S*ister Genevieve. She was my sixth-grade teacher at St. Mathieu's School in Fall River, Massachusetts. She got kicked out of the South in the 1960s because she organized a biracial communion service. She was no radical, but she taught me more than anyone else about racial justice without saying much of anything.

—*E. J. Dionne Jr., syndicated columnist, Washington, D.C.*

*D*on Hoff, who was the football coach at Bloomfield Hills High School in Michigan. He was a when-the-going-gets-tough kind of guy and he was totally unlike the rest of us. He was as wide as he was tall, and he had no neck, and arms like tugboats. He drove us mercilessly. It was the first time any of us had to really work. We loved it. We all used to throw up after practice. That was great, too.

—*Dennis A. Dinan, Woods Hole, Massachusetts*

# *I Remember . . .*

$\mathcal{M}$y mom. I had her twice as a teacher in the College Charlemagne, once in grade six and once in grade ten. She was a really good teacher—fair to all. Sometimes too fair from her daughter's viewpoint.

—*Danielle Shannon, flight attendant, Calgary, Alberta*

$\mathcal{M}$ohammad Donago, my algebra teacher in Iran. He knew his subject but, more important, he knew his students, and he understood what we knew and thus taught us at our level.

—*Fereshteh Nejad, dental assistant, Washington, D.C.*

$\mathcal{M}$rs. Aageson, my fifth- and sixth-grade teacher. We so admired and looked up to her. And then she invited a bunch of girls over to her house for lunch. That was a very big deal. It meant we were important.

—*Karen Froslid Jones, St. Paul, Minnesota*

# *I Remember . . .*

*F*red Zimmerman, who taught journalism and English at Washburn College in Topeka. He opened the joys of reading up to me. He told us stories about the great reporters in American history. He made me a romantic.

*—Harry Middleton, former director, Lyndon B. Johnson Library, Austin, Texas*

*M*rs. Kaufman, my kindergarten teacher at Georgetown Day School. For her, everybody was special, everyone was included. And when she died a few years ago, everybody went to her memorial service and sobbed. We all thought we were Mrs. K's favorite.

*—Deborah Ann Fanburg, marketing consultant, Bethesda, Maryland*

*M*rs. Kauser. She was my teacher freshman year in high school, and she was Jewish. She taught us all about the Holocaust. She was the first person who ever taught me about evil.

*—Kirby Dorrell, salesman, Austin, Texas*

# ℐ Remember . . .

𝒵arm Geisenhoff, who taught humanities to high school seniors. She was a dynamo, a force of nature, in constant motion. We had a daily two-hour class in an historic one-room schoolhouse on the grounds of a big high school in St. Paul, Minnesota. She poked and prodded until we learned to think—and speak—for ourselves. No one could just sit there. You had to participate, and it had to be well thought out. I think many of us who went through her class consider it a life-changing experience. You just looked at the world differently after she opened your eyes. I acquired a lifelong love of art history from her, for which I will always be grateful.

—*Ellen Edwards, journalist, Washington, D.C.*

𝑀r. Rainer, my high school British literature teacher. He taught us Shakespeare mainly by conveying his incredible love for it. He taught high school kids Middle English. He colored the way I looked at things and read things and heard things the rest of my life.

—*Candace Kaller, art collector, Bethesda, Maryland*

# $\mathcal{I}$ $\mathcal{R}$emember . . .

$\mathcal{M}$ulford Q. Sibley, the controversial, tall, gray-haired professor of political theory at the University of Minnesota. I entered his class as a nineteen-year-old who had been warned against being unduly influenced by a man who was a pacifist and who stood against war long before it became popular during Vietnam. His antiwar efforts during World War II earned him the wrath of Minnesota. He was a socialist and spent his entire life as a prophet both ahead and behind his times. But Professor Sibley was a teacher, a scholar, and a human of great integrity. He only asked us to read the texts, understand the ideas, treat them with respect, and draw our own conclusions. He asked only that we respect ourselves and our ideas enough to live in accordance with them. He may have been without honor as a prophet, but I have had no better teacher.

—*Dale Kuehne, political scientist, St. Anselm College, Manchester, New Hampshire*

$\mathcal{M}$rs. Best. She was my first-grade teacher, my music teacher, and my Sunday school teacher in Arlington, Virginia. We lived in the same neighborhood and she taught me the truth of life at age five.

—*Velma Tinner, associate executive director, Metropolitan Washington, D.C., YMCA*

# I Remember . . .

Dennie Edelbrock, who taught me the trumpet. He was one of the best in the world. He knew what a trumpet player should know. He changed my attitude completely about music. He made me competitive in music.

—*Zac Gomez, band leader, Washington, D.C.*

Mrs. Blankenship, my fourth-grade teacher at Parsons Grade School. She was friendly. She talked to us about all kinds of stuff. She made us know that if there was something bothering us we had someone to talk with.

—*Debbie Crossland, state park employee, Canaan Valley, West Virginia*

Professor Zolnowski, economics professor at Mount St. Mary's College. Economics can be a bore, but he made it interesting and fun. He joked around like crazy. We didn't notice what was happening, but we were learning like crazy. I aced that class.

—*Curtis Ray, tire-store manager, Bethesda, Maryland*

# ℐ Remember . . .

𝒩at Halpern, who taught me how to play golf. He was a bachelor curmudgeon in his late sixties, his face was leathery and unshaven, he always had a cigar in his teeth, and he would bark in gravelly New Yorkese, "You're doin' dis here," and exaggerate my flawed swing. Back in the 1950s, because I was young I was barred from an earlier tee time, and I would carry my bag to the first tee after all the adults had teed off. One afternoon Nat asked me to join him. He played each weekend morning with the only three men who would tolerate his company, returning to the first tee after lunch to play another nine or eighteen alone, repairing the morning's flaws. But that tentative meeting became a pattern, and he took me under his wing. I absorbed every word, and we eventually formed a generation-skipping partnership that won a pairs tournament. Even today, after some errant swing, I hear his gruff reproach: "You're doin' dis here."

—*Paul K. Schwarz, teacher, White Plains, New York*

𝓜iss Gregory, my geography teacher in Addlestone in Surry. I had no interest whatsoever in geography. She made me love it.

—*Jane Jenkyn, business manager, Chertsey, England*

# ℐ Remember . . .

ℳr. Bijlsma, the teacher in my little village school in Holland. He empathized with the students who didn't understand their lessons. That helped me as a teacher.

—*Geert Hekman, retired teacher, Calgary, Alberta*

ℳiss Bleedhorn, my eighth-grade teacher at Mark Twain Elementary School in South Dakota. We called her "Blood and Guts." She was tough as hell. She had the courage to give out bad grades. But if you had any ambition at all in Sioux Falls, you thanked her for what she did for you.

—*John W. Mashek, writer, Washington, D.C.*

ℳiss Smith, who taught accounting at Dr. Norman Bethune Collegiate High School. She made me realize that when a teacher is taught, the student learns more.

—*Karen Albanesi, word processor, Scarborough, Ontario*

John Hennessy, who was my senior-thesis adviser at Dartmouth. He gave me self-confidence and convinced me I could determine my own path. I recently had a reunion with him. He remembered every detail about me.

—*Karen Francis, automobile executive, Detroit, Michigan*

Donald Hafner, a political-science and international-relations professor at Boston College. He didn't care as much about publishing as he did about teaching, and that made all the difference in his teaching.

—*Mary Ellen Joyce, Brookings Institution, Washington, D.C.*

Richard W. Leopold. He was a professor of history at Northwestern. I have never met a professor so intensively interested in what students thought. When you wrote something for him he would return it with comments in different colors of ink—one for syntax, one for content, one for style. He would read our papers the way we should have read his books.

—*Timothy Walch, director, Herbert Hoover Library, West Branch, Iowa*

# *I Remember . . .*

*E*mmit J. Hoolihan, who was a band teacher at Temple City High School in southern California. He was enthusiastic and he always had life-building statements for us. He used to say that any idiot could march but it takes a special kind of idiot to do it right.

—*Greg Hanzel, cartographer, Washington, D.C.*

*M*arie Natoli, a professor of political science at Boston College. I took a media and politics class with her. I was sort of interested in the media and sort of interested in politics when the course started. I was really interested in both of them when the course ended.

—*Anne Gavin, director of the Massachusetts office of Federal/State Relations, Washington, D.C.*

*S*am Adams, who taught at the Harvard Business School. He taught finance. He made something brilliant and even compelling out of something that was confusing and repellent.

—*Richard A. Oppel,* editor, Austin American-Statesman, *Austin, Texas*

# I Remember . . .

Arthur G. Hughes, the chairman of the English department at the Culver Military Academy in Indiana. He was a great towering guy with hair like Van Cliburn. He was a huge man, a god. He seemed to see in me great things that I didn't see. He made me think I was somebody.

*—Andrew H. Malcolm, writer, Helena, Montana*

Miss Armstrong, my English teacher at Jefferson Junior High in Washington. I was failing. I was failing bad. But she stuck with me until I got it together. She put the clamps on me—and I passed.

*—Earl Patrick, gym attendant, Washington, D.C.*

Mr. Clark, my biology teacher in freshman and sophomore year in high school. He taught us through demonstration and by example. He taught above our heads, but he never lost our attention.

*—Dean Hassen, director of information systems, Whole Foods Markets, Chicago, Illinois*

$\mathcal{M}$s. Owens, who was my English teacher at Mount Vernon High School. I got kicked out of my original English class because I was too rowdy and too rude. I egged on the teacher and was put into Ms. Owens's class and—suddenly—I was an English student. She made me do better than I thought I could.

—*Mary Beth Lane, interior designer, Great Falls, Virginia*

$\mathcal{M}$iss Stella. She taught in the second grade at St. Francis School in Natchez, Mississippi. I can see her right now, so many years later. I remember how we used to go on recess and eat a caramel candy called the Slo Poke. It lasted all day. She didn't mind if we sucked on it—as long as we did our work.

—*Jackie Thornburg, secretary, Austin, Texas*

$\mathcal{B}$rother Philip. He taught Algebra II at St. John's High School in Washington. I always hated math. But he made it lively. I actually began to love math.

—*Robert Welch, firefighter, Washington, D.C.*

# *I Remember . . .*

*My* English teacher at West Springfield High in northern Virginia. Those were the days when we were all free-form, and she was, too. We were all hippies, and she wore long gauze dresses. She was very innovative, getting us involved in stuff we otherwise would have avoided.

—*Leslie Mehl, ski-store manager, Canaan Valley, West Virginia*

*Mrs.* Brioli, my third-grade teacher. She was so kind, so nice, so warm. It's amazing, but though it's been years I can still feel her warmth.

—*Kelly Franks, medical secretary, Bethesda, Maryland*

*Page* Keeton, a law professor at the University of Texas. I was not a student, and most of the teachers were not much in the way of teachers, but Page Keeton just swept us along.

—*Robert S. Strauss, former chairman, Democratic National Committee, Washington, D.C.*

# ℐ Remember . . .

ℬarbara Trujiloo, my fourth-grade teacher in Albuquerque. She did whatever she wanted to do and taught us whatever she was interested in, which was a lot. She was learning with us and was so enthused by what she was learning that we were, too. She was the teacher who turned me around.

*—Dorie Lawson, lecture agent, Rockport, Maine*

𝒯im Rowley, who taught business strategy at the University of Toronto. He challenged me to think—in a very different way. He didn't just say: "Think for yourself." He exposed us to the difficulties inherent in real inquiry and encouraged us to think for ourselves.

*—Baljit Salh, management consultant, Etobicoke, Ontario*

𝒨ildred Hayes, my first-grade teacher. I wasn't a particularly eager student and was very shy and was put in a first-grade class with people I didn't know. I tried to get my mother to get me out of that class. But Miss Hayes watched over me and told me I could be a great student. I've never forgotten it.

*—James McGovern, congressman, Worcester, Massachusetts*

# *I Remember . . .*

$\mathcal{M}$rs. Morrison, my fifth-grade teacher in Vancouver, Washington. When you are eleven and twelve years old you go through self-doubt. But Mrs. Morrison taught every single one of us to be proud of ourselves.

—*Sara Tuominen, flight attendant, Vancouver, Washington*

$\mathcal{B}$etty Stitt, my French teacher in Austin, Texas. I wound up living in France and was an interpreter on overseas air flights. I was paid to talk—all because of her.

—*Sharlet Hoium, special-education teacher, Chicago, Illinois*

$\mathcal{J}$oyce Koury. She taught music at Shaw Junior High School in Swampscott, Massachusetts, and she cared about the material she was teaching and the kids she was teaching. She tried hard to instill a love of serious music in all of us, and every time I go to an opera I know she succeeded.

—*Robert M. Halperin, lawyer, Washington, D.C.*

# ℐ Remember . . .

𝒟on Junkins, who taught English at the University of Massachusetts. He was remarkable. He was less interested in having us find ourselves than in teaching us the things we needed to know.

*—Drew Johnson, cashier, Book People, Austin, Texas*

𝒫eter Breit. He taught political science at the University of Hartford. He demanded that we do more than we thought we could.

*—Zoe Donan Gedal, analyst, Washington, D.C.*

𝒟avid Morgan, my fifth-grade history and math teacher at Monongah Middle School. It was a tiny school in West Virginia. And Mr. Morgan set me on track to get a complete, well-rounded liberal arts education. But there's one thing I remember about him: He knew everything.

*—Heath Olson, sports-store technician, Canaan Valley, West Virginia*

*H*erbert O. Reed, who was my constitutional-law professor at Boston College Law School. It was 1969. Nothing had quite prepared me for him. This was a black professor teaching white middle- and working-class students. He had been Muhammad Ali's lawyer in the draft-dodging case. He was involved in the Chicago Seven trial. He had been Adam Clayton Powell's lawyer. And he explained to us that the most important thing you have to know about the Constitution is that from this point forward the Fourteenth Amendment—the equal-protection amendment—will be used to animate every other section of the Constitution. That one idea, which ran contrary to the way constitutional law had been taught, colored the way I looked at the Constitution from that day forward.

—*Edward Markey, congressman, Malden, Massachusetts*

*F*ather Bonaventure, who taught me history for four years at Bishop Egan High School in Levittown, Pennsylvania. He taught me to go one-on-one with the world. He taught me to look beyond Levittown.

—*Kevin Gleason, framer, Washington, D.C.*

*M*abel Swisher, my seventh-grade English teacher in St. Mary's, West Virginia. She was a stickler—proper grammar, proper English. But by the time we got out of school we knew how to speak and write.

*—Jennifer Neelon, administrator, St. Mary's, West Virginia*

*D*r. Crisswell, my A-level history teacher at King George V School in Hong Kong. He was a great big fat man and he would swing back and forth and tell great historical stories. He was very much a character himself. He taught English history in a very non-English setting, and yet it seemed so real.

*—Ailsa Auchnie, editor, BBC Radio, London*

*E*lena Ivanovna, my German teacher at School No. 22 in Izhevsk, Russia. She made learning languages so much fun that I felt that I had to learn lots of them. She was the reason I picked up English so quickly when I came here.

*—Rouslan Khamidoulline, video store manager, Washington, D.C.*

# 𝒯 𝑅𝑒𝑚𝑒𝑚𝑏𝑒𝑟...

𝒟r. Sangermano, my biology teacher at Masconomet Regional High. He had a nontraditional way of teaching. He knew how to relate. He knew his customers. He used humor to good effect. I use some of his sappy sayings to this day.

—*Nat Howe, store manager, North Conway, New Hampshire*

𝑅ichard Berkner, my political-science professor at Shippensburg College who taught me an important lesson about our democracy. I vehemently opposed the Vietnam War, but I had begun to despair that it would ever end. I began to question whether democracy worked. I'll never forget what he said: Democracy does work and when enough people in the country opposed the war, the government would act. He was right. Too often we assume that democracy doesn't work unless it is working the way we want it to. In fact, democracy works when the majority of people want it to and care deeply enough to get involved.

—*Jeanne Shaheen, governor of New Hampshire*

# *I Remember . . .*

$\mathcal{M}$rs. Daoust, my grade two teacher outside of Toronto. That was a year of transition. We were expected to handle a lot more and not be like a baby, and she treated us like we were responsible children. By doing that, she helped make us responsible.

—*Mary Gooderham, writer, Ottawa, Ontario*

$\mathcal{M}$arie Day, my music teacher in Smithfield, Virginia. She took so much time with me. She was never negative. She was a dynamite person. As a person, she made music seem even bigger, even greater, than ever.

—*Betty Wise, assistant principal, Deal Junior High School,*
*Washington, D.C.*

$\mathcal{M}$r. Gardner, my sixth-grade teacher at Greg Rogers Elementary School in Chula Vista, California. He rescued me from a bully one time. If it hadn't been for him, Daniel Sneed would have beaten me up.

—*Tod Jones, English professor, University of Maryland*

# I Remember . . .

Wayne E. Stevens. He taught me colonial American history in college. He was dry and colorless, but he had integrity, a bearing, a manner, that had a great deal of influence on me. To me he represented the nature of the scholarly world.

*—Edward Connery Lathem, editor of the Robert Frost poems, Hanover, New Hampshire*

Mr. French, who taught science at Barnstable Middle School on Cape Cod. He was not put off by a student like me who questioned authority at every turn. He found a way to keep me in the classroom anyway.

*—Mara Rudman, former deputy assistant to the president for national-security affairs, Washington, D.C.*

Warner Moss, who taught political science at the College of William and Mary. He made me think.

*—Barbara Littell, Brookings Institution, Washington, D.C.*

𝒫rofessor John Rassias, who taught me French in my freshman year in college. I'm sure I should remember what he said about modern French theater. Instead, I remember him whipping a T-bone steak at a room full of students. He yanked us on stage and made us dress in ridiculous costumes. For our final class, he re-enacted a death scene, stabbing himself with a rose. We cheered. We hugged. I didn't mind the ketchup that sprayed from the stage wound all over my sweater.

—*Sara Hoagland Hunter, writer, Weston, Massachusetts*

𝒮teve Statuto, my marketing professor at Boston College. He told me I should go to law school. I hadn't even considered that. My family was in the auto business. So I went home and talked with my father and my grandfather. My grandfather liked the law school idea; he figured he'd save on legal bills. I might have ended up in politics in the end anyway, but going to law school made a difference. It changed my direction.

—*Paul Cellucci, U.S. ambassador to Canada, Ottawa, Ontario*

# *I Remember . . .*

$\mathcal{D}$an Purrington, who was an astronomy professor at Tulane. Two nights a week we went to his class, and it was a real gut. He recycled all the material and all the tests. The first test, everybody got an A. Then he stood up in front of the few of us who came to class after the first week and told us not to tell anybody, but he wasn't going to give the same old test the next time. So when he gave the second test you could hear all the fraternity guys say, "Did you ever see this question before?" A lot of guys didn't get into medical school because of this, and what recourse did they have? They couldn't go to the dean. I learned more from that than from any other course I ever took.

—Mark Manuel, *vice president, Crown Equipment, New Bremen, Ohio*

$\mathcal{M}$rs. Thomasetti, a preschool teacher in Uxbridge, Massachusetts. She wasn't my teacher, but she was my son's teacher. He was speech-delayed. Mrs. Thomasetti was great with him. Within a year there was real improvement. She was the kind of teacher who made a lasting impact on a student, and on his mother.

—Cheryl Potochnick, *housekeeping inspector,*
*Center Conway, New Hampshire*

# *I Remember . . .*

*B*ob Jamieson, who taught English at Haverford School. He hated me. He was a Harvard man, one of those 1950s prep-school teachers in a somewhat seedy sport coat. He was incredibly demanding. I was a so-so student. But he knew there was something inside me and he made it come out.

—*Albert R. Hunt, panelist,* The Capital Gang, *Washington, D.C.*

*J*oy Lou Thompson, who taught math at Harman High School. She wouldn't let us use our fingers for math. She made us use our brains.

—*Paula Teeter, receptionist, Whitmer, West Virginia*

*C*oach Killen, the swim coach at Wilson High School in Washington. He knew that physical education was an entertainment business.

—*Mike Fabrikant, teacher's assistant, Wilson High School, Washington, D.C.*

# *I Remember . . .*

*E*rnest Knaggs, my junior high school science teacher in Davis, West Virginia. He didn't teach us by formula, he taught us by example, and some of them were outrageous. Outrageous! But he really imprinted the principles of science in our minds.

—*David Collins, retired coal miner, Davis, West Virginia*

*R*ev. Charles Curran, my professor at SMU's School of Theology. I took his course "The Christian, the Church, and the Public Good," and he taught that the church should use its First Amendment rights to work for a more just society and the public good, but not at the expense of the separation of church and state. He reinforced in me the importance of being ethical and true to yourself, no matter the consequences.

—*Ed Wisneski, associate athletic director, Southern Methodist University, Dallas, Texas*

*J*ohn T. Spillane, my government-affairs teacher in high school. He tuned me in to the whole political process. We don't agree on politics. We agree on the importance of politics.

—*Andrew H. Card Jr., White House chief of staff, Washington, D.C.*

101

# I Remember...

$\mathcal{M}$arion Just, who teaches political science at Wellesley College. Going to a place like Wellesley sometimes makes you feel you're at a shrine of knowledge. She demystified the shrine and taught me I could learn.

—*Mary Konsoulis, curator, Washington, D.C.*

$\mathcal{M}$y junior high school assistant football coach. This was in Teaneck, New Jersey, and I was an overweight offensive guard with no particular talents. I had dreams of being Joe Namath and none of the ability, and at five foot four no prospects. Coach came up to me during a game—I was second-string—and asked me if I could throw a block. The assistant coach said, "Hell no, he's a pansy." I didn't get into the game, and from that day forward I realized I would never be motivated by negativity. He taught me a great lesson.

—*David Black, literary agent, New York, New York*

# I Remember . . .

*M*rs. DeCarlo, who taught the seventh and eighth grades at Pickering School in Salem, Massachusetts. That's the age when kids slack off. She made us go up a notch. She took our faults and made them advantages.

—*John Tierney, congressman, Salem, Massachusetts*

*P*erry Meisel. He was a rather mad professor of English literature whose brilliance brainwashed me at NYU. He seemed to be able to articulate thoughts that I had but could not enunciate myself. He was always five steps ahead of where I wanted to be. He told jokes that I understood only days later. He was volatile, frightening, intimidating—and brilliant.

—*Gary Morris, literary agent, New York, New York*

*M*rs. Cowles, a special-education teacher at Bethlehem Elementary School. I had a learning disability and she encouraged me to work hard at overcoming it. I still have that disability, but she helped me make great progress.

—*Tawnya Tanqueray, cashier, North Conway, New Hampshire*

# $\mathcal{I}$ $\mathcal{R}$emember . . .

$\mathcal{R}$oger Lane, my history professor at Haverford College. He was a very relaxed guy but he was demanding. I wound up spending a lot of time with him, and I learned something from every minute.

—*Macy Nelson, environmental lawyer, Baltimore, Maryland*

$\mathcal{H}$azel Nenni, my English teacher during senior year at Matewan High School in West Virginia. She was very strict. There was no nonsense permitted. But she knew what it would take to succeed in life and made sure we were equipped for success.

—*Gene Kitts, consulting engineer, Charleston, West Virginia*

$\mathcal{D}$r. Helga Welsh, who taught politics at Wake Forest. She challenged me. She forced me to expand. She forced me to think. She made me critical. I no longer take everything as fact.

—*Matt Harrington, researcher, Greensboro, North Carolina*

# *I Remember . . .*

$\mathcal{C}$olonel Brine. He was a teacher at Selwyn House School, a boys' private school in Montreal. When I was a miserable student, just about failing out of school, he kept me behind at school twice a week even though I made no improvements whatsoever. But the following year I became a good student, and there is no question that the work this man did in helping me focus, concentrate, and learn how to study made all the difference in the world.

—*James Stein, developer, Montreal, Quebec*

$\mathcal{M}$iss O'Connell, who taught fifth grade at Midland Street Elementary School. She was the classic Irish beauty with the porcelain skin and with her hair in a French twist. She was thin and always looked so proper, but she had a flair that I couldn't help but notice—and that perked me up. My father died when I was not quite four years old, and I was an only child. So I was lonely. But I made a lot of friends that year because Miss O'Connell took a personal interest in me and gave me self-esteem.

—*Merri I. Baker, press gallery aide, Capitol Hill, Washington, D.C.*

# $\mathcal{I}\,\mathcal{R}emember\ldots$

$\mathcal{M}$argaret Hennig, who taught marketing and retailing at Simmons College. She really noticed me, and she really encouraged me to do a lot more than I would have thought. She told me I could go to business school—at a time when very few women did that. She really made a difference.

—*Cheryl Howard, marketing specialist, Winchester, Massachusetts*

$\mathcal{K}$evin Sanborn, an anesthesiologist at Columbia College of Physicians and Surgeons. He was approachable, unlike so many other professors in medical school. He was also knowledgeable and very down to earth. Not everyone who is smart can share what he knows, but he could.

—*Jacqueline A. Bello, neuroradiologist, New York, New York*

$\mathcal{J}$ohn Yothers, my visual-arts teacher in high school in Pennsylvania. He got me thinking about the arts and encouraged us in very subtle ways to make us think. I didn't know how to think creatively until I met him, and I use his methods to teach my own students now.

—*Kim Williams, teacher, Culpeper, Virginia*

# *I Remember . . .*

*M*iss Heatherman. I had her for English and for Latin at Lowell High School. She was an older woman, probably near sixty-five. She was really tough. I still think of Miss Heatherman every time I use certain vocabulary words, like *bombastic*. She actually made us do the homework every day. She called on all of us every day. She was brutal on people who were not prepared. Later on you would learn that was important.

—*Martin Meehan, congressman, Lowell, Massachusetts*

*M*y art teacher at Amerigo Vespucci School in Napoli. He taught me the discipline I need at the stove. He also taught me the creativity. And he taught me that you need them both.

—*Jerry Castiglia, chef-owner of an Italian restaurant, Keyser, West Virginia*

*M*rs. Cirbus, my third-grade teacher in Staten Island, New York. She was very kind, she had a very good sense of humor, and she actually helped us develop our thinking. She was very methodical, but she was very gentle. I'll always remember her.

—*Diane Conocchioli, accountant, Washington, D.C.*

# *I Remember* . . .

*E*unice Guill, who taught English in high school. She was prim and proper. She started out the year being very firm, scaring us a little. But as the year wore on you felt the warmth and love of teaching that radiated from her. She so loved to teach that she made us love to learn.

—*Dianne Conwell, homemaker, Richmond, Virginia*

*D*ale Brentrup, who taught me architecture at the University of North Carolina in Charlotte. He nurtured my excitement for sustainable design. He had the knowledge, but he also made me believe.

—*Christopher Tiernan, architect, Portsmouth, New Hampshire*

*M*arie Collins, my high school English teacher. She was enthusiastic and encouraging. She made me keep a personal journal; she read it and handed me back suggestions and critiques. She made me understand that writing—not only the required book review on *Jude the Obscure* but outside writing—was the key to thinking.

—*David Graulich, publicist, San Francisco, California*

# *I Remember ...*

*M*r. Creighton, my English teacher at Fort Frye High School in Beverly, Ohio. He supported girls' sports at a time when no one did. He'd put signs on our lockers, leave gifts and candy and poems for all of us. It got so that we began looking for this stuff before every game. He was way ahead of his time, but he made sure we knew that at least one man believed that girls should have sports teams, too.

—*Cathy Morgenstern, nurse practitioner, Marietta, Ohio*

*G*ary Becker, who taught me economic theory at Columbia. He won a Nobel Prize and is quite conservative. He taught by throwing questions to us. I didn't buy his politics but I bought his belief that economic tools could be used to analyze many problems. The whole world has come to believe in this, but to us in 1966 this was a great, and important, insight.

—*Robert D. Reischauer, president, Urban Institute, Washington, D.C.*

*J*ospehine Polito, my sixth-grade teacher in Auburn, New York. She challenged me to rise above what I wanted to do.

—*William Fulton, regional planner, Ventura, California*

*G*erda Kalman, who was one of my teachers at Salem High. She taught freshman Western civilization and Russian history. Her enthusiasm and dedication were impressive. But her great skill was understanding—really understanding—individual students' strengths and weaknesses. She knew how to critique, push, and encourage students—and to turn weaknesses into strengths.

—*John E. Sununu, congressman, Salem, New Hampshire*

*H*enry Bedford, chairman of the history department at Exeter. He was a great man and he made me feel important. For the first time in a class I was not only dealing with grown-up issues, I felt like a grown-up.

—*David Eisenhower, senior research fellow, University of Pennsylvania*

*D*r. Lefkowitz, my organic-chemistry teacher at Suffolk University in Boston. If he didn't know the answer to something he wouldn't give us bull. He'd find the answer. I respected him for what he didn't know.

—*Richard Vento, digital-imaging salesman, Culpeper, Virginia*

# *I Remember* . . .

*P*hil Gonyar, who taught an advanced history and government course called "Foundations in American Freedom." He was the first person who really gave me a real thrill about how this country got started and how important it is to participate in it. People always ask me if I wanted to be governor when I was a kid. The truth is, until I took his course, all I wanted to do was play for the Celtics.

*—John R. McKernan Jr., former governor of Maine*

*B*etsy Webb, who taught gym in Harman, West Virginia. She was a nice, polite person. She taught kids in all grades, kindergarten through twelve. No one does this anymore, but she did it with good humor. And she knew all our names.

*—Katy Harper, group-travel coordinator, Job, West Virginia*

*M*r. Morey, who was my math teacher at East Bridgewater High School in Massachusetts. He kept the class interested. Some of us were strong in math, some weak, but he made us all feel equal in class.

*—Joyce Brothers, office manager, North Conway, New Hampshire*

# *I Remember . . .*

*D*avid Bartholomew, my ski teacher. He understood all the things your body had to do but, more than that, he understood how to explain it all to us.

—*Janet Preston, attorney, Canaan Valley, West Virginia*

*M*r. Park, my middle-school teacher in Korea. School there is very difficult, far harder than here. He was a hard teacher, but he knew when to be soft.

—*Jung Il Park, cab driver, Boston, Massachusetts*

*H*. Daniel Peck, my English professor at Vassar. He taught American literature in an unforgettable way—by taking the paintings of the Hudson River School and integrating the art into the literature. He was able to show how literature flows from many sources.

—*Kate Myers, attorney, Washington, D.C.*

𝒮ister Mary Byron, my high school English and French teacher at Notre Dame High School in Clarksburg. She's now a canon lawyer for the church. It didn't matter what she taught; she always taught with a great deal of fun. She made the world accessible.

—*Julia Aucremanne, saleswoman, Clarksburg, West Virginia*

𝑅einhold Niebuhr, who taught me at Union Seminary in New York. I was in the church before I fell from grace and went into politics. I would take long walks with him on Riverside Drive in New York and listen to him talk like a machine gun. His philosophy of history made more sense to me than any other I ever encountered. He had an understanding of the sinfulness of human nature but also the infinite possibility of human existence.

—*Bill Hudnut, former mayor, Indianapolis, Indiana*

# I Remember . . .

$\mathscr{M}$rs. Keanelly, who taught social studies at Raynham Junior High School in Massachusetts. She was interactive before *interactive* was a word. She was one of those teachers who made you feel you were in control of your own grade. If you wanted to do it well, all you had to do was work hard. She made a big deal about working hard, and then—at this awkward age when everybody was afraid to stand up in front of the class—she made you feel proud to get up in front of everyone.

*—Michael Meehan, political operative, Washington, D.C.*

$\mathscr{J}$effrey Diamond, who taught chemistry at Bunker Hill Community College. I was born in Ethiopia, and he was very patient with me. He had the ability to explain everything and to understand why we could not understand.

*—Abraham Jerry, cab driver, Boston, Massachusetts*

$\mathscr{D}$r. McDaniel, my high school government teacher at Jeb Stuart High in Virginia. I hate government. I couldn't care less about politics. But she loved it—and helped me see why.

*—Jose Lopez, aquatics teacher, Falls Church, Virginia*

114

# *I Remember . . .*

*E*ric Goldman, who taught History 301 at Princeton. He was a terrific writer and an even better lecturer and teacher. I don't think he knew me. More than anybody else, he gave me something that has lasted my whole lifetime: an interest in what is going on in the world.

—*Harold Pachios, lawyer, Portland, Maine*

*K*athy Abberman, who taught at Carlisle High. She put in real time and real effort. She tutored me for my SATs and years after high school helped me get into graduate school. She did her job with a passion. She was unforgettable.

—*Greg Thomas, carpet salesman, Carlisle, Pennsylvania*

*M*rs. Peace, an elementary school teacher in a southeast Texas town called Jasper. It was a small, rural school. More than anything I remember the way she read to us in class. It made me always love to listen to stories.

—*Pam Johnson, administrative assistant, Dallas, Texas*

# *I Remember . . .*

*V*ivian Smith, my math teacher in South Hill, Virginia. She was very strict and she had very high expectations. Everyone was afraid of this lady, and so of course I had to get an A in her class. I just had to. And I did. She was a great personality.

—*Clemontene Rountree, science teacher, Washington, D.C.*

*S*ister Mary Evangeline, my sixth-grade teacher at Immaculate Conception School in Indian Orchard, Massachusetts. She had a huge influence on me. She taught me how to learn and how to have self-esteem. She was a very strong woman who wanted to produce very strong people.

—*Mary Dougal, ophthalmologist, Northbrook, Illinois*

*M*r. O'Connor, my seventh- and ninth-grade teacher at Burnt Hills–Balston Lake Junior High School in upstate New York. He was a very strict teacher. He commanded every last kid's respect. But he gave his kids—us—just as much respect. We really learned from him.

—*Dan Lewis, sporting goods store operator, North Conway, New Hampshire*

# ℐ Remember . . .

*E*nos Held, who taught science at Swampscott High School. It has been forty-five years and I still remember how much I hated science. But he made science pleasant. He did it by making science personal.

—*Norman A. Goodwin, shoe salesman, San Francisco, California*

*M*rs. Moore, my sixth-grade English teacher at El Rodea School in Beverly Hills. She really respected grammar. With her we diagrammed sentences. We drilled. We paid attention to words. We learned that there was no such word as *gotten*.

—*Frank Mankiewicz, public-relations executive, Washington, D.C.*

*H*oward Ziff, who taught at the University of Massachusetts. He showed me how important passion is in one's life and studies. His application of passion was broad: He was passionate about principle and ethics and the need to apply those things. I was your basic college student and, because of him, I realized that you have to really feel things deeply and that, to have fun in life, you have to have impact.

—*Larry Carpman, consultant, Boston, Massachusetts*

$\mathscr{M}$r. Werkhauser, my accounting teacher at Clearwater High School in Florida. He realized I didn't need to follow the curriculum. He gave me the freedom to finish school eleven weeks early. He knew enough to let me learn at my own speed.

—*James Huber, Wendy's restaurant manager, Parsons, West Virginia*

$\mathscr{M}$iss McDonald, my second-grade teacher at Oyster River Elementary School in Durham, New Hampshire. I came out of that classroom with a sense of well-being that I never lost.

—*Shaula Levinson, homemaker, Portsmouth, New Hampshire*

$\mathscr{M}$iss Doll Means. She taught English at Charleston High School in Charleston, Arkansas. At that time Charleston's population was 851 and we didn't have running water or electricity. But Miss Doll's grammar was a force among those 851 people. Her grammar was as precise as a math equation. One day she had me read *Beowulf* in front of the class. She said: "Doesn't he have a fine voice? Wouldn't it be a tragedy if he doesn't use those talents and that voice?"

—*Dale Bumpers, former senator, Little Rock, Arkansas*

Terry F. J. Mills, who taught grade seven in Westmount, Quebec. He had a receding hairline and sculpted features and was famous for his hyperbole. He would spend whole classes spinning tales, most of which were untrue. He would tell us about building the DEW Line or single-handedly pulling a car out of a ditch or eating twelve slices of roast beef at one sitting. He understood how to draw kids in, and we listened with rapt attention. But he knew what he was doing. He was opening up for us a whole world of fantasy.

—*Andrew Cohen, writer and teacher, Ottawa, Ontario*

Gaston Banco, a secondary school teacher I had in Uruguay. He was supposed to teach advanced-level Spanish. He spent 95 percent of the time talking about anything but Spanish: film, politics, Vietnam. We were in Uruguay, after all, and so we had Spanish knocked cold. Three weeks before the exam he put us to work at Spanish. We did fine. But the things that mattered to me were the things we talked and learned about before we worried about the exam. He challenged our assumptions.

—*Michael Chu, venture capitalist, Boston, Massachusetts*

# ℐ Remember . . .

𝒱era Paul Humphrey. I loved and idolized many of my teachers, but she was the most memorable. She taught the first and second grades at Mount Kisco Elementary School in New York. She was an older woman and a born teacher. She played the piano and did art. She had beautiful handwriting, and she did the attendance with a pen she dipped in a bottle of ink. For her the accoutrements of teaching were so glamorous. She knew us better than we knew ourselves. And she was so memorable that forty years later I walked past a woman on the street and said, "She's wearing Vera Paul Humphrey's perfume."

—*Valerie Tripp, writer of the American Girl series,*
*Silver Spring, Maryland*

ℳr. Thompson, my American history teacher at Delaware Academy in Delhi, New York. He took us on class trips. He was a big figure in our lives—bigger than life. He was knowledgeable, of course, but he also had a booming voice. He intimidated us into doing the work.

—*Roz Fitch, educational conference coordinator, Washington, D.C.*

# I Remember . . .

Mrs. Engleman, my English teacher at Linden High School in New Jersey. She was very interested in her students. I had her for ancient Greek literature. I still remember the *Iliad* and *Odyssey*. I wouldn't have remembered a bit of it without her.

—*Cris Cormier, flight attendant, Derry, New Hampshire*

Mrs. Sleight, my math teacher at New Trier High School. I was a good math student but I was a boisterous kid. I was going through puberty with a lot of energy and she called my bluff. She forced me to have discipline. With a combination of harshness and heart, she forced me to be quiet and to listen and to learn something. She was like a commandant, but she was my commandant.

—*Barry L. MacLean, manufacturing executive, Mattawa, Illinois*

Mrs. Simms, my algebra teacher at Einstein High School in Kensington. For us, algebra was a chore, but for her it was never a chore. She did the impossible. She was pleasant every day of the year.

—*Eddie Shah, tire mechanic, Damascus, Maryland*

# ℐ Remember . . .

ℳr. Wolk. He was a speech teacher at Roosevelt High School in Minneapolis. If you were late to class, he'd greet you at the door-way with a challenge: "Why don't you give a two-minute speech on, say, eggs?" He taught us how to think on our feet, organize information, and present it with impact. I wish I had kept bet-ter notes on how to do all those things.

—*Sandra McCalvy, administrative assistant, Minneapolis, Minnesota*

ℳarguerite Strehlau, who was my fifth- and sixth-grade teacher at Poughkeepsie Day School. She remained my lifelong friend. She made everything totally alive for me. She fostered my imagination. She took us everywhere, she taught us the American Revolution, she even read to us. I still cherish the books she read to us.

—*Jud Sommer, managing director, Goldman Sachs, Washington, D.C.*

ℳr. Dixon, who was my English teacher in seventh and eighth grades at Landon School in Bethesda, Maryland. We called him "Daddy Dix." I had a lot of shenanigans at that age and he han-dled me by making me read.

—*Arthur Smith, banker, Washington, D.C.*

# *I Remember* . . .

*H*arold Spaeth, an expert in politics and the judiciary whom I got to know at Michigan State University. He was a brilliant professor, but he was from Cincinnati and Detroit and had no connection at all with the outside world. And he was no country boy. But it was clear at a dinner party once that he believed carrots grew on trees. He was absolutely convinced of that. We all berated him at dinner, and he finally backed down. It was the only time I ever saw him bow to pressure.

—*Michael Haselswerdt, political scientist, Buffalo, New York*

*M*rs. Dillon, my fifth-grade teacher at Hurld School in Woburn, Massachusetts. She used to always give me math problems with 2s and 9s in them. I have a learning disability and I'd write the numbers backwards. She taught me that just because I was a little different didn't make me different.

—*Peter Toye, auto-service supervisor, Bethesda, Maryland*

*M*y physics teacher in high school in Rockville, Maryland. He let us blow stuff up.

—*Jared Farber, merchandise promotions officer, Rockville, Maryland*

## *I Remember...*

*P*rofessor Geohegan, who was a religion professor at Bowdoin College. This was 1962, before *diversity* was the watchword. He talked about the world's religions as if we were a part of all those religions. He taught us that to understand any one religion we had to understand all religions. Pretty good lesson.

—*Christian Potholm, political scientist, Brunswick, Maine*

*M*r. Robertson, my high school physics teacher at Hurricane High School. He was a mean old guy but at the end of the year everyone loved him. He was a father figure for us all.

—*Vanessa Reed, physical therapy assistant, Hurricane, West Virginia*

*C*hris Henderson, my civil-engineering professor in college. He made a difference for me. He made me want to be a civil engineer. That never worked out. But I still follow civil engineering and Chris Henderson's work.

—*Paul Smith, nuclear-power-plant engineer, Shippenport, Pennsylvania*

# $\mathcal{I}$ $\mathcal{R}$emember . . .

$\mathcal{M}$rs. McGuire, my ninth-grade English teacher in Buena Vista, Virginia. She was very innovative, really ahead of her time. She used music and poetry to teach us how to write. It worked.

*—Bryan Hoos, owner of a convenience grocery store, Roanoke, Virginia*

$\mathcal{M}$r. Eagen, my English teacher in Newport, Rhode Island. He knew how to deal with a classroom of randy teenage boys very well. He encouraged me to write and to read. He gave me an abiding interest in American literature and the taste for going a little bit out of the mainstream in my writing.

*—Richard Maiman, political scientist, Portland, Maine*

$\mathcal{M}$arian Duffett, my high school English teacher. She was always present to our concerns, as if she were one of us. But she was a great teacher because she inspired us to think beyond ourselves.

*—Diane Winston, foundation program officer, Philadelphia, Pennsylvania*

# *I Remember . . .*

Professor Miller, a swashbuckler who taught me American and European history at what used to be Montana State University. I had a lot of professors—I speak in the plural—who gave me the benefit of the doubt and got me through. But he knew I had great interest in history and geography and helped me organize those interests.

—*Mike Mansfield, former Senate majority leader and ambassador to Japan; Missoula, Montana*

Mrs. Nowlin, my twelfth-grade English teacher in San Antonio. She took me under her wing as a writer. She said one thing I always remember: Write what is in your heart.

—*Lisa Cruz, publicist, San Marcos, Texas*

Ms. Glayt, my fifth-grade teacher at Warner Avenue Elementary School in West Los Angeles. She got me to read the newspaper and to learn about the world. Otherwise I would have stayed in my sheltered existence and known nothing about anything beyond my own neighborhood.

—*Vicki Torf, graphic artist, Ventura, California*

# I Remember . . .

Fred Morhart. He was my history teacher at West Potomac High School in Alexandria, Virginia. He also went to my church. He let us revise our papers until they were perfect. In doing that, he let us know that he would stick with us until we were perfect.

*—Brooks Preuher, urban planner, Arlington, Virginia*

Julia Murphy. She was my high school Latin teacher in Rumford, Maine. I took three years of Latin from her. She impressed upon us the importance of the classics in our lives. They had influenced the whole world, and her argument was that they should influence us, too, even if we were in a small rural town. She made us think we were living amid the Roman wars.

*—Severin Beliveau, lawyer, Augusta, Maine*

Roger Bergstrom, my high school speech and drama teacher. He taught me how to write and outline and make a speech. I didn't think I needed to know that. But now I make a ton of speeches and because of him I know how to do it.

*—Angus King, governor of Maine*

$\mathcal{M}$r. Cabe, history teacher at Eisenhower Senior High School in Yakima, Washington. The first test I got an A. The second test I got a B. He called me in after class and asked me what was the matter. I told him that a B wasn't bad. He looked me in the eye and made me believe there was no excuse for not getting an A on a single test. And there wasn't a single test from then on that I didn't get that A. It was an extraordinary moment to have someone believe in me like that.

—*Dan Larson, lobbyist, Washington, D.C.*

$\mathcal{M}$rs. Meadows, my third-grade teacher in Monahans, Texas. She was married to the principal. She taught us that learning was not something to resist. She made it feel that she was in the business of learning along with us. She loved learning and she loved teaching us to love it, too.

—*T. Cay Rowe, media relations specialist, Wimberley, Texas*

$\mathcal{V}$elma Davis, who taught English and Spanish in high school. Her enthusiasm for good grammar and for reading became my enthusiasms. She made me want to read more than the Hardy Boys.

—*Thad Cochran, U.S. senator, Jackson, Mississippi*

# *I Remember . . .*

$\mathcal{M}$r. Horton, my twelfth-grade teacher at Cranston High School. He was too strict a teacher for many kids, too strong, but for me he was gentle. I wasn't the brightest kid and I wasn't the stupidest kid. I didn't feel like doing much as a kid, though. But he got me to work.

*—Wayne Gambugo, cab driver, Brighton, Massachusetts*

$\mathcal{M}$y math teacher at P.S. 126. When I emigrated from Korea I went directly into the New York public schools. The language barrier was so great that when I took a true/false test I didn't know the meaning of *true* or *false*. I mixed them up. So I got every one of the answers wrong. The teacher figured out that I knew the material and he gave me a 100 on the exam.

*—John Lee, anesthesiologist, Marietta, Ohio*

$\mathcal{J}$ules Chametsky. He taught Elizabethan poetry at the University of Massachusetts. I was eighteen or nineteen and he allowed me to become his friend. Teachers weren't supposed to do that, and he did.

*—Bob Levey, Brookline, Massachusetts*

# *I Remember . . .*

*Grace* Cullen, an English teacher at Outremont High School in Quebec. She acted out everything she read. She bubbled. She made Shakespeare and Dickens seem as if they were occurring in our own classroom. She also made me believe that recess and gym didn't have to be my best subjects.

—*Marcia Schnaar, administrative assistant to the Montreal Expos,*
*Montreal, Quebec*

*Dr.* Lee Bowen, my history teacher in my junior year at Boston College. He was a convert to Catholicism, very learned, very personable, even to the point of inviting groups of us to his home for long discussions. He gave Catholicism an intellectual basis. It was not just piety that he taught. It was the history of the church infused with intellectual life. He put Christianity together intellectually for me.

—*Father Robert F. Drinan, law professor and former congressman,*
*Washington, D.C.*

Margaret Hayes, who taught American history in Newtown High School in Queens. Neither of my parents even went to high school. But Mrs. Hayes gave me a sense that one could go beyond college, to be thoroughly trained in American history. Some years ago I was invited back after forty years to the school to be inducted into the hall of fame. I wanted to say a word or two about her, thinking that no one would remember her and that she was long gone. A few days later I got a blue envelope with scented paper. Inside was a letter. It began, "Dear William . . ."

*—William Leuchtenburg, biographer of Franklin Roosevelt,*
*Chapel Hill, North Carolina*

Constance Miller, an art teacher in Avon, Massachusetts. Today they would call her a mentor. That idea wasn't around those days. She was a great guiding force not only in art but in literature and drama. She had a broad definition of "art" and she leaned us toward being classy instead of just being a regular kid.

*—Patty McCarthy, administrative assistant, New York, New York*

# *I Remember . . .*

*I*ndch Howland, who taught eurythmics at the Oberlin Conservatory of Music. She was an Apache and she was deep into ethnic music, and she taught classical music by showing that it came from basic ethnic impulses. She gave me insights I've never forgotten.

—*Major Timothy Foley, director, United States Marine Band,*
*Washington, D.C.*

*M*iss Nagel, an exchange teacher from New Zealand who spent some time with us at the normal school in Eau Claire, Wisconsin. She allowed the kids to indulge their creativity. That year we made a model of a Greek home. I still remember it as one of the biggest challenges of my life.

—*Jeanne Phillips, Dear Abby columnist, Los Angeles, California*

*J*. L. L. J. Llewellyn, who taught me at law school at the University of Toronto. He taught in the old style, extracting concepts from examples. A lot of the other professors were businesslike. He made us think.

—*Liz Breen, lawyer, Toronto, Ontario*

# *I Remember...*

*S*ister Susannah, my sixth-grade teacher at St. Joseph School in South Bend, Indiana. I was a little wild in school. She almost flunked me, but she passed me from the sixth grade to the seventh "on trial." That meant that I had six months to cut it in the seventh grade. Sounds funny now, but do you think that didn't affect my whole life?

—*John McMeel, publisher, Kansas City, Missouri*

*C*. S. Lewis, my fifth-grade teacher in Huntsville, Texas. He was an acerbic but brilliant teacher. Almost everything I know in my life about geography I learned from him, and not only where the Strait of Magellan and the Bay of Fundy are. He was a great one for thumping us on the head if we got things wrong. But he took such pride in me that I began to take pride in myself.

—*Arthur Wiese, energy executive, New Orleans, Louisiana*

*D*ickie Hall, my ski instructor in Vermont. He used intuition to teach this very intuitive sport. He taught me how to telemark ski—and how to teach others to do it.

—*Chip Chase, manager, White Grass cross-country ski center,*
*Canaan Valley, West Virginia*

*J*erome Liebling, who taught film and photography at Hampshire College. We had a true master/student relationship. He was the guiding spirit of my professional career. And I remember the first time we had a difference in filmmaking. He made a suggestion. I resisted. He suggested again. I kept resisting. And when he stopped pushing back at me I knew I was on my way.

—*Ken Burns, filmmaker, Walpole, New Hampshire*

*M*y second-grade teacher. She knew I liked to write. One day I was really restless, walking around, not paying attention. Then she gave us an assignment. We had to write something, and I wrote about walking around. She pulled me aside and said, "Why don't you learn the word *meander*?" I went home with a great new word and a great new attitude.

—*David Wade, New Haven, Connecticut*

# *I Remember . . .*

*S*ister Joselma, a nun I had in the third and fifth grades. She was just out of the novitiate and teaching her first class, and she was a young nun. That was something special because all the other nuns were ancient. But we were young, too, and she was kind to us.

—*Mary Jane Loras, administrative assistant, Philadelphia, Pennsylvania*

*M*rs. Geisler. She was my fifth-grade teacher at St. Matthew's School in Buffalo, New York. She introduced me to Henry David Thoreau. That led me to force my parents to take me to Walden Pond and Concord, Massachusetts. I was ten years old. It's still the vacation and the book and the teacher I remember the most.

—*Cynthia L. Skrzycki, writer, Washington, D.C.*

*S*urely many of you have your own stories about teachers whose voices still speak to you, whose faces still smile (or scowl) upon you, whose lessons still breathe with you. Please feel free to send your own stories for a second volume of *I Remember My Teacher*. The only requirements are that the entries begin with the phrase "I remember . . ." and that they be brief. All entries are subject to mild editing, and all submissions become the property of the author of this book. Please include your name and day and evening telephone numbers and send them to:

David M. Shribman
1130 Connecticut Avenue, Suite 520
Washington, D.C. 20036